YES, BUT IS IT GOOD FOR THE JEWS?

YES, BUT IS IT GOOD FOR THE JEWS?

JONNY GELLER

A BEGINNER'S GUIDE VOL. I

ALLEN LANE
an imprint of
PENGUIN BOOKS

ALLEN LANE

Published by the Penguin Group
Penguin Books Ltd, 80 Strand, London WC2R ORL, England
Penguin Group (USA) Inc., 375 Hudson Street, New York, New York 10014, USA
Penguin Group (Canada), 90 Eglinton Avenue East, Suite 700, Toronto, Ontario, Canada M4P 2Y3
(a division of Pearson Penguin Canada Inc.)
Penguin Ireland, 25 St Stephen's Green, Dublin 2, Ireland (a division of Penguin Books Ltd)
Penguin Group (Australia), 250 Camberwell Road, Camberwell, Victoria 3124, Australia
(a division of Pearson Australia Group Pty Ltd)
Penguin Books India Pvt Ltd, 11 Community Centre, Panchsheel Park, New Delhi – 110 017, India
Penguin Group (NZ), 67 Apollo Drive, Mairangi Bay, Auckland 1310, New Zealand
(a division of Pearson New Zealand Ltd)
Penguin Books (South Africa) (Pty) Ltd, 24 Sturdee Avenue,
Rosebank, Johannesburg 2196, South Africa

Penguin Books Ltd, Registered Offices: 80 Strand, London WC2R ORL, England

www.penguin.com

First published 2006
1

Copyright © Jonny Geller, 2006

The moral right of the author has been asserted

Set in 11.5/14pt AGaramond
by Palimpsest Book Production Limited, Grangemouth, Stirlingshire
Printed in England by Clays Ltd, St Ives plc

ISBN-13: 978-0-713-99959-4
ISBN-10: 0-713-99959-4

For
Karen, Ben and Joe
– good for this Jew

'Anyone meshugge enough to call himself a Jew is a Jew.'

David Ben-Gurion (first prime minister of Israel)

the word 'bad', we merely say 'not good' – after all, we've had 5,000 years of bad things happening to us, why not be a little more positive?

This first book of a fourteen-volume cycle of works will outline the basic principles of Judology, using selected examples in alphabetical order to guide the novice in the practicalities of this science.

To aid the serious student of Judology on his or her path (yes, women are allowed to delve into the secrets of this reclusive sect) to perfect understanding, the author has provided maps, graphs, lists and discussion topics. As with all Jewish academic endeavour, we at the Judological Institute of Spiritual Mathematics, or JISM, welcome your input and refer you to our website isitgoodforthejews.com, where discussion forums encourage debate on issues discussed in the book.

Who is a Jew? The editor defines this as one who has at least one Jewish parent and/or grandparent. In fact, just use the Nuremburg Laws of 1935 as a reliable guide – if it was good enough for Hitler, it's good enough for us.

One final note: please do not borrow this book from a friend or a library, as borrowing is not good for the Jews. Buying is.

AUTHOR'S NOTE

'As long as there have been Jews, there has been Judology'
    (Rabbi Chelm of Bratislaw, *Judaica Numerolis*, 1648)

Judology is undeniably one of Western civilization's oldest branches of the sciences. This short book cannot hope to do justice to the libraries of scholarship on the subject. The author merely wishes to bring the principles and some applications to the forefront of interested, curious minds.

Judology, like all mystical philosophies, has had its critics. Described as 'arcane, diffuse and frustrating' by its *bête noire*, Professor Amos Avla (*Judology Is Fake*, Manischewitz Press, 1928), the science was driven underground for more than seventy years until the latter part of the twentieth century.

What is Judology? In brief, it is a cousin of mathematics, a sister to the Talmudic art of Gematriya – apportioning numerical value to individual letters in the Torah and thereby giving them mystical significance – a third cousin of Kabbalah. It is, at heart, a spiritual guide to the complexities of Jewish identity. Happily, this study, which was previously restricted to male Jews over the age of forty-seven who had undergone circumcision twice, is now open to you, the hungry reader.

The Judological Institute of Spiritual Mathematics (JISM) is, for the first time, prepared to share its mathematical formula with the outside world. This is a highly controversial move, and a rift occurred in the Annual Conference of Judology in the autumn of 2005, when Solomon Pinkas, the dean of the Solomon Pinkas Academy of Spiritual Mathematics (SPASM), expelled members who voted in favour of sharing our findings with the world. A schism in SPASM led to the formation of JISM in 2006. We at the Institute believe there is too much secrecy in this world, and it is time for Jew and non-Jew to work together and join forces in the process of determining whether something is good or not good for the Jews. Less *Opus Dei*, more *Och an Vey*.

In his informative 1927 book, Professor Ivor Broygus, MBris, Yd, defines Judology as 'the numerical attribution or evaluation of whether something, animate or inanimate, is good for the Jews' (*Tzoyrus by Broygus*, Paranoid Press, 1927). The author owes a supreme debt of gratitude to this monumental work, now sadly out of print, and wishes to refer any complaint, charges of libel, upset or accusations of defamation to the offices of Professor Broygus' publishers, Paranoid Press, 23 Gramercy Park, New York, NY10002.

JG
March 2006
at his home in a secret location

HOW JEW ARE YOU?

Before embarking on our journey, perhaps take a moment to answer the following questions to determine if YOU ARE GOOD FOR THE JEWS.

1 Your only daughter brings home her new boyfriend from her gap year in America, and they declare their intention to wed in the traditions of her new man's family – that of the Native American tribe of the Cherokee. His name is Adahy, which means 'Lives in the Woods'. Do you:

a) welcome them into your home, prepare a lovely meal and quietly retire to the bathroom, where you slit your throat;

b) announce you are changing your name too – to 'Sitting Shiva';

c) accept the style of the wedding as long as you can choose the caterer?

2 It is Christmas time, and little Mendle, your five-year-old, asks you why Jews don't have Santa Claus. Do you:

a) tell him in a kind, gentle voice that Santa Claus is, in fact, based on Baron Herman Von Claus, a famous Bavarian anti-Semite who poisoned Jewish children;

b) tell him, Santa Claus is a lie, but don't mention it to Big Dave at school or he will beat you to a pulp;

c) Tell him that you put a sign on the chimney saying, 'Keep Out! Jews Live Here'?

3 You are invited to your boss's home for dinner. He is serving the hors d'œuvres, melon and ham. Do you:

a) discreetly slip the ham under the tablecloth when nobody is looking;

b) convince yourself it must be kosher meat that just looks like ham and tastes like wurst;

c) say loudly that you are Jewish and you have always suspected your white boss of being a racist, particularly since his imitation of the Black and White Minstrels' classic 'Pack Up Your Troubles' at last year's Christmas party?

4 Your favourite team is playing on Yom Kippur. Do you:

a) ask 'What is Yom Kippur?';

b) pretend you have a headache and leave shul to watch it in the quiet and privacy of your own home;

c) Sky Plus the game and watch it after the breaking of the fast?

5 The Six Day War is:

a) the third Arab–Israeli conflict conducted over six days in 1967;

b) a normal working week for orthodox Jews;

c) the usual timeline it takes to get over a fight with your spouse.

6 You are choosing a holiday. Do you:

a) think about it, skim the brochures and then book Eilat, like every year;

b) check out whether the country voted for or against the creation of Israel in 1948;

c) not bother – the food is always awful and they speak in such funny accents?

7 You have been invited to the barmitzvah of the son of a relative whom you haven't spoken to for many years due to a family broygus, the cause of which you can't remember. Do you:

a) attend the simcha and lavish generous gifts on the unsuspecting barmitzvah boy;

b) attend the function, eat and drink as much as you can, stuff your pockets full of leftovers and free cigars and leave, giving him a fiver;

c) fall out with every family member over whether you should attend, induce an ulcer and insomnia, go and have a miserable time?

8 Chasidism is:

a) a bunch of meshugganehs who screw through a sheet;

b) a revolutionary movement founded in the eighteenth-century Pale of Settlement that introduced joy to devotion in religious Judaism;

c) I loved *Yentl*.

9 You are invited to join the local reading group, where you will be the only Jew in the club. Do you:

a) say how much you love the works of Trollope, so everyone knows you are not too Jewish;

b) say no to every suggestion until somebody eventually suggests either Primo Levi or Howard Jacobson?

c) The price of books these days, I'd rather wait for the movie.

10 Circumcision is:

a) a ritual that orginates with Abraham's covenant to God and a symbol of Jewish commitment to a spiritual life;

b) a snip off the old block;

c) very common these days: which porn star can you name that hasn't been circumcised?

A = 3 points   B = 5 points   C = 7 points

If you scored 30–40 points, you are NOT GOOD FOR THE JEWS. Do you mix enough with Jews? Why not join your local bridge club as a start?

If you scored 41–55 points, you are clearly a Jew with self-hating issues. You are NOT GOOD FOR THE JEWS. No advice available.

If you scored 56–70 points, you are a balanced, integrated Jew who is ready to enter the first stage of Judology. No advice needed.

THE MATHEMATICAL FORMULA

Here, for the first time, the secret formula to determine whether something is good or not good for the Jews will be revealed. It must be noted that if an entry is defined as 'not good' it does not necessarily mean that as such it is bad for the Jews. It is merely not a positive force for Jews. In certain cases, it can simply be Jew-neutral and therefore simply not good and not bad.

Important note
Each category is marked out of 7, the most important number for Jews. According to the Laws of Judology, the determination of how this mark out of 7 is reached can only be disclosed to someone who knows all six orders of Hillel's Mishna, backwards, and in Cockney rhyming slang. The number 7 is important in many religions, none more so than Judaism. For example:

7 days in the week
7 planetary spheres
7 Wonders of the World
7 fat cows eat 7 thin cows in Pharaoh's dream

Moses wore size 7 sandals
7 deadly sins
7 graces
7-year itch
7th month in the Jewish calendar marks the start of the
new year
7 seas
7 dwarfs
7 courses served in an average Jewish Friday-night dinner

The Formula

Anti-Semitic potential (otherwise known as backlash) [1]
+ impact on the world [2]
x the j-factor [3]
= tzurus [4]
÷7 (the mystical Kabbalistic number) [5]

0–7: not good for the Jews
7.1–7.99: borderline, therefore probably not good for
the Jews
8–14: good for the Jews

So, for example:
Easter

backlash	+ impact	x j-factor	= tzurus	÷ kabbalah	= good/not good
7	+ 6.2	x 3.35	= 40.87	÷ 7	= 5.84

Therefore Easter is not good for the Jews.

[1] Clearly there is anti-Semitic potential in everything, so this category is hard to evaluate. We have restricted this to mean an open and obvious threat to the Jews. So, violence resulting from the subject will score 7; slight fear of anti-Semitic backlash will score 1. This will be known as 'backlash'.

[2] This indicates whether the subject has spawned imitators/imitations or movements outside the orginal impact of their intentions. The effect will be judged by the lasting impact ('lasting' defined as ten years or more) made outside the United Kingdom. This will be known as 'impact'.

[3] Defined as any link whatsoever the subject has to Jewish heritage, culture or matrilineal descent, or whether the subject is open about his or her Jewishness or whether the subject is known as being particularly 'Jewish'. The higher the grade, the more overt the Jewish identity. We have refused to look back further than seven generations. This will be known as 'j-factor'.

[4] Tzurus is Yiddish for troubles, the default position of world Jewry. Tzurus is the effect of backlash potential spread across the world having been increased by Jewish origin. This will be known as 'tzurus'.

[5] The mystical Kabbalistic number 7 will be known as 'kabbalah'.

ALCOHOL According to Fogwell's Guides, alcoholic liquor is one of the basic constituents of wine. Alcohol is a tasteless and colourless chemical that occurs naturally during fermentation when sugars from grape juice are processed by yeast. The alcohol content of wine ranges from about 8 to 14 per cent by volume.

* * *

Wine and religion have a long history together. Many medieval monks throughout Europe had a major sideline as vintners. Jews are commanded to have at least four full cups on Passover (some argue that it is the only way to get through the interminable Seder service) and on Purim – the festival to commemorate the survival of Jews from genocide – Jews are ordered to get as drunk as skunks. The commandment on Purim is quite specific: no beer or spirits, just wine, and only at the daytime Purim meal. One custom even decrees that a Jew should drink 'until he does not know' the difference between Mordechai (their loyal leader) and Haman (the evil tyrant). If every time Jews commemorated escape from near-extinction by getting drunk, there would be a lot of pissed Jews on the tube.

A story: Rabbi Samuelson crashes into the car of Father Mulranney. Miraculously, neither cleric sustains any injury. In fact, not a scratch is to be found on either of them. Both cars are wrecks. 'Surely a sign from Hashem?' Rabbi Samuelson declares. 'To be true – the hand of God,' agrees Father Mulranney. 'Even more miraculous,' says the Rabbi, 'is this unbroken bottle of Palwin 4a kosher wine in my boot.' He opens the wine and passes it to the priest, who takes a few swigs. The rabbi then throws the bottle away. 'You not having any?' the priest asks. 'Nah, I'll wait until the police arrive,' the rabbi answers.

Aside from the Purim clause, the Bible takes a rather unsympathetic view of alcohol. Drunkenness was punishable by death (Deuteronomy 21:20–21); Lot was seduced by his own daughters when they'd had a few too many Tia Marias (Genesis 19:33–6); King Solomon the Wise was convinced his wisdom came from a bottle, so he was shicker a lot, poor fellow; Noah got so drunk that when he was discovered, naked, by his son Ham, the unlucky boy was cursed; Aaron's two sons were killed for officiating as priests while drunk; and so on.

For non-Jews it is different. Jesus turns water into wine at Cana (John 2) and thus begin two millennia of alcoholism among priests. Traditionally, Jewish member-only golf clubs demand higher fees to compensate for the lack of income they would normally get from non-Jews at the bar. If you read the Bible, wouldn't you be terrified of drinking?

One true story: a Hasidic rabbi invites a new member to his home for Shabbos dinner after the service. The rabbi is widely known for his piety and his absolute belief that every commandment in the Torah must be practised. He offers the new congregant a whisky before the meal, but the member declines politely, saying, 'Sorry, Rabbi, I'm driving.' Sometimes, a Jew should shut up and drink.

---

backlash + impact x j-factor = tzurus ÷ kabbalah = good/not good
3.1   + 7   x 4.5   = 45.45 ÷ 7   = 6.49

☀ **ALCOHOL IS NOT GOOD FOR THE JEWS.**

AMISH, THE A Christian sect of about 145,000 people who live in settlements across the US and Ontario, Canada but are found mostly in Pennsylvania, Ohio and Indiana. They are the descendants of Swiss Anabaptists (later known as Mennonites), who later broke from the Church to follow Jacob Ammam in the 1600s. They moved to America in the eighteenth and nineteenth centuries to escape hard times and persecution in Europe. They will not embrace modernity. They speak a dialect of German called Pennsylvania Dutch. (Source: padutch.com.)

♦ ♦ ♦

The Amish and the Hasidim have much in common. Both share a penchant for the ancient art of facial hair sculpting and both have been depicted in mainstream cinema. The Amish were portrayed sympathetically in *Witness* (1985) by the sumptuous Kelly McGillis. The Hasidim were depicted shamefully in that *dreck* movie *A Stranger Among Us* (1992), with the pneumatic Melanie Griffiths. Hardly a fair fight.

The similarity in looks between the Lubavitchers and the Amish can be of use if you happen to be a Hasid being chased down a Pennsylvanian street by a horde of Jew-haters. Shout a few choice phrases in Pennsylvania Dutch to distract your pursuers and they will stop in their tracks and offer to help you on to the back of your cart.

Consider this famous story: a woman on a bus in the Midwest was overheard abusing a young man dressed in black hat, black coat and with a long dark beard who happened to sit next to her. 'Jews like you,' she spat. 'I'm sorry, madam?' he said. 'Look at you. All in black, with your thick coats in the height of summer and your ridiculous hats! It's Jews like you that give the rest of us a bad name.' He replied calmly, 'I beg your pardon, madam, but I am not Jewish. I'm Amish.' The woman looked back and smiled, 'How nice. You've kept your customs.'

---

backlash + impact x j-factor = tzurus ÷ kabbalah = good/not good

3.7   + 2.2   x 2   = 11.8 ÷ 7   = 1.7

✺ **THE AMISH ARE NOT GOOD FOR THE JEWS.**

ASHAMED OF YOUR NAME? JEWS WHO SWITCHED

Cardinal Jean-Marie Lustiger changed his name from **Aaron Lustiger**. Yes, the former Archbishop of Paris is in fact a Jew. For a moment, the world's first bona fide Jewish Pope was a possibility. Sadly, the German non-Jewish Joseph Ratzinger beat him to the post after Cardinal Lustiger's mentor, John Paul II, died in 2005.

Robert Zimmerman changed his name to **Bob Dylan** when he realized the closest thing to Jewish folk music was klezmer, and there ain't no money in klezmer. He also changed religions for a brief spell when he became a born-again Christian in 1979. This proved a bad career move, as his two 'Christian' albums, *Slow Train Coming* and *Saved*, were, well, shit. Religiously he redeemed himself with his pro-Israel song 'Neighbourhood Bully' on his 1983 album *Infidels*. He was later photographed at the Western Wall in Jerusalem wearing a skullcap.

Albert Einstein changed his name to **Albert Brooks**. No, not that Albert Einstein. What kind of parent does this to a son? Nobody can blame Albert Brooks, the actor, writer and director (*Broadcast News*, *The Muse*), for changing his surname. It is doubtful whether this was motivated by shame of being Jewish – more likely by fear of daily humiliation in the playground.

Melvin Kaminsky changed his name to **Mel Brooks**. **Allen Stewart Königsberg** changed his name to **Woody Allen**. Makes sense – after all, the last thing these young comedians needed was people thinking they were Jewish. No future in that.

Ralphie Lifshitz changed his name to **Ralph Lauren**. The son of a house painter, young Ralphie realized early on that there was no future in fashion with a dentist's name. Imagine people buying Dolce and Gabinski or Georgio Armanilovitch. Doesn't work.

Jonathan Stuart Leibowitz clearly felt it paid to sound Scottish rather than Jewish and discreetly removed the conspicuous surname to become **Jon Stewart** and found fame in America on *The Daily Show* as a result.

Leonard Alfred Schneider changed his name to **Lenny Bruce** because he thought Schneider was 'too Hollywood'.

Issur Danielovich Demsky changed his name to **Kirk Douglas**, which is probably the most dramatic name switch in history, as 'kirk' means 'church'.

Paul Simon and **Art Garfunkel** did not change their names! Perhaps they thought referring to Jesus in their hit song 'Mrs Robinson' would get them off the hook. Their first hit was, however, under a pseudonym of Tom and Jerry, but their Columbia Records producer Tom Wilson was furious when they suggested that their names were too Jewish. He insisted they couldn't sing about racial injustice but try not to appear 'too Jewish'.

BAGEL, THE A bread product made from yeasted wheat dough shaped as a ring that is boiled and then baked. The bagel is said to have originated in 1683, when a Jewish baker from Vienna created them as a gift to King Jan Sobieski of Poland to commemorate the King's victory over the Turks in that year. Immigrants in the 1880s brought the bagel to New York City, from where its popularity spread to Europe.

◆ ◆ ◆

The bagel is clearly the greatest export for the Jews since the Old Testament. In Russia, the bublik has become so mainstream that most Russians aren't aware that it was originally a Jewish bread. The fact that people in many countries that are steeped in anti-Semitism enjoy the bagel and do not know it was created, developed and distributed by Jews makes this category all the sweeter.

The bagel has also been a symbol of philosophical difference. Rabbi Plotz of Pinsk, the famous biblical commentator, said, 'The non-Jew sees the bagel, the Jew sees the hole.' However, it has been pointed out that the baker charges for the bagel, hole or no hole.

---

backlash + impact x j-factor = tzurus ÷ kabbalah = good/not good
3.05   + 5.45 x 6.9   = 58.65 ÷ 7   = 8.38

 THE BAGEL IS GOOD FOR THE JEWS.

BEE, THE SPELLING A national institution in America, the National Spelling Bee is in its seventy-ninth year. Administered by E. W. Scripps, this annual event was first introduced in 1925 and is now so popular that it is televised and attracts a huge audience. Contestants must be fourteen or younger and must first win their state championships before they can go on to represent their state at the national competition. The 1999 Bee was covered in the Oscar-nominated documentary *Spellbound* (2002), directed by Jeff Blitz.

◆ ◆ ◆

The National Spelling Bee is screened on the cable channel ESPN, so it must be a sport – and a sport Jews can actually win! All it needs is the magic Jewish combination of a nerdy, bookish pre-pubescent and a very pushy parent. Slam-dunk, if you ask me. For the spectator there is also the added joy in seeing a Gentile from Iowa really, really trying to spell the word 'Lubavitcher'. Judologists take the Spelling Bee extremely seriously as a recruiting ground for potential candidates for the Judological Institute of Spiritual Mathematics (JISM), as we are always on the hunt for students of the Word. If every letter in the Torah has numerical significance, and every word several meanings, then spelling is pretty important to the Jews.

It is not all one way, and Jews' knowledge of their host nation and culture is also tested. In some ways, the Spelling Bee can be seen as a subtle, coded, discreet way of testing citizenship. For example, was there an anti-Semitic agenda when Harry, a Jewish kid from New Jersey, was eliminated from the competition after he failed to spell the word 'banns' correctly (shown in the documentary *Spellbound*)? How was he to know this word for the religious announcement of a marriage – a word that orginated from the Catholic Church?

For those worried about an Aryan slant to the questions, recall that the 1983 final word was 'Purim' (source: somethingjewish.co.uk). But surely, anyone who cannot spell this word, denoting the time when Jews were threatened with annihilation, may well be an anti-Semite? Sensitivities reached fever-pitch when the *San Francisco Chronicle* got into trouble after publishing a test poster for the Bee. In test example number 10 the word 'disproportionate' was used in the following context: 'Israel came under heavy international criticism for the Gaza offensive. UN Secretary-General Kofi Annan and others questioned whether it had been a *disproportionate* response to the use of crude Qassam rockets by Palestinian militants.' Jewish groups clearly saw this as a coded calling card for Hamas. The paper later apologized.

---

backlash + impact x j-factor = tzurus ÷ kabbalah = good/not good
5.04   + 5.4   x 6.2   = 64.7 ÷ 7   = 9.24

 # THE NATIONAL SPELLING BEE IS GOOD FOR THE JEWS.

BEWITCHED Over 250 episodes of this sitcom ran from 1964 to 1972. Samantha (Elizabeth Montgomery) and Darrin (Dick York and Dick Sargent) are a nondescript couple living in a Connecticut suburb, she a housewife, he an advertising executive. Samantha is a witch, but she promises her husband that she will not use her magic at home and will be a good, normal wife. She proves unable to do this as her numerous eccentric relatives pop in to cause chaos in every episode. In 2005 a movie version was released, with Nicole Kidman as Samantha, Will Ferrell as Darrin and Shirley MacLaine as Samantha's mother, Endora.

Exodus 22:18: 'Thou shalt not suffer a witch to live.'

• • •

Bewitched is the prototype of all American sitcoms. It also presents a fascinating dilemma for the Judologist. An assimilationist fantasy or a Jewish expression of identity? America was still reeling from the effects of McCarthyism when *Bewitched* began production, and Jewish writers had to be careful how they expressed their views, so it is worth examining the possible subtext or semiotics of this ground-breaking sitcom.

Assimilationist Fantasy. Although no Jewish actors appeared on screen in the main roles, *Bewitched* was created by Sol Saks and directed by William Asher. Other Jewish writers and directors on the show included: Ron Friedman, Bernie Kahn, Milt Rosen, Jack Sher, Fred Freeman and Lawrence J. Cohen, Jerry Mayer and Paul L. Friedman, Sherman Marks, Alan Rafkin and R. Robert Rosenbaum. Even the recent movie was written, directed and produced by Jews.

William Asher was married to Elizabeth Montgomery (Samantha), and the picture of the small, balding Jewish-boy-made-good together with the slender, Waspish, all-American blonde could have been taken straight from the pages of *Der Stürmer*. Marrying out has never looked so good.

In fifties America the Great Jewish American Dream was the picket fence, the job in advertising or insurance and the Shiksa wife waiting at home. There are even the slightly annoying next-door Jews, Gladys and Abner Kravitz, to make the picture perfect. Jews should be close but not too close. However, the hidden subtext is that the lovely blonde at home is, in fact, a witch. Being accepted is hard. In the episode 'The Battle of Burning Oak', the chairman of the exclusive Burning Oak country club proposes Darrin for membership, but Samantha's humble ancestry ruins their chances of breaking into this American pure-bred elite. A heartbreaking *cri de cœur* of the Jewish experience?

Jewish expression of identity. On the other hand, perhaps Samantha is the Jew? From Darrin's point of view, he has an overbearing mother-in-law who is a big *macher* in the witches community. She disapproves greatly of his marriage to her daughter and she hates seeing Samantha suppressing her witch identity to fit in with her mortal husband (read Goy) and his mortal concerns (gaining membership of exclusive clubs). Samantha just wants to be like everyone around her and for people to accept her as one of them. Trouble is, her community, her family, her heritage and her own innate witchness just keep surfacing. And when her children are born, there is no denying that they have inherited her powers – matrilineal descent.

Remember too that her power resides in her nose.

Bewitched also contains a subliminal mysogynist message, namely, you keep your wife stuck in the kitchen for long enough she turns into a witch and, worse, her mother.

---

backlash + impact x j-factor = tzurus ÷ kabbalah = good/not
4.68   + 3.4   x 5.7   = 46.1   ÷ 7   = 6.6

✹ ***BEWITCHED* IS NOT GOOD FOR THE JEWS.**

BIBLE, THE

Old Testament

Written between 1400 and 100 BC, the Old Testament (also called the Hebrew Bible or Tanakh) is a collection of five books of Moses, eight books of Prophets and eleven books of writings. The Pentateuch, or Chumash, is the principal five books of Moses, which detail the story of the Hebrews as they left slavery and founded their own country in Israel, the land promised to them by God, according to the Torah. The creation of the world is described in the first book, Genesis.

❖ ❖ ❖

Without these books there would be no Jews, so it is hard to argue that the five books of Moses are bad for the Jews. The 613 commandments, however, are way too many rules: 248 laws dictating what you should do and 365 saying what you can't. No wonder Jews have been criticized for being bossy control freaks. With that much *nudging*, who wouldn't be a bag of nerves?

Also, the laws on animal sacrifice are excessive in this day and age.

Terms like 'Chosen People' do not help either.

---

backlash + impact x j-factor = tzurus ÷ kabbalah = good/not good

7   + 7   x 7   = 98   ÷ 7   = 14

☀ THE OLD TESTAMENT IS GOOD FOR THE JEWS.

New Testament

The New Testament or Greek Scriptures is a collection of twenty-seven books written after the life of Jesus Christ. The New Testament was written over a 100-year period between AD 50 and 150 and covers the life and teachings of the Son of God, according to the Christian Bible. There are many authors of these books, but the primary sources are the Gospels written by Matthew, Mark, Luke and John.

•   •   •

Jesus was a Jew and was named the Jewish King even at his crucifixion, so there are strong arguments to defend the New Testament's place in the pro-Jew pantheon, but troublesome sections such as Matthew 27:25, which states, 'Then answered all the people, and said, His blood be on us, and on our children' and John 19: 6,15, which shows the Jews shouting, 'Crucify him', did not help the successful integration of the Jewish people into the Christian world.

However, the authors of the Gospels – with the possible exception of Luke – were all Jews, so, unless they were the first self-haters in history, they could just have been complaining about the Jewish authorities rather than Jews as a whole. Many notable passages ascribe blame for Jesus' execution to the Jewish Sanhedrin, so maybe the fault does lie with the administration. Having said this, the Roman procurator Pontius Pilate is portrayed as a puppet of the unruly Jewish crowd and the powerful Jewish lobby, who were bent on shaping policy to suit their own nefarious ends. Some things don't change . . .

Jews in the New Testament do not come out of it well unless they are converting to Christianity, otherwise it is said that 'salvation is from the Jews' (John, 4:22). Hard to argue that the Good News Bible is Great News for the Jews.

---

backlash + impact x j-factor = tzurus ÷ kabbalah = good/not good
7   + 5   x 3.5   = 42   ÷ 7   = 6

✺ THE NEW TESTAMENT IS NOT GOOD FOR THE JEWS.

BIG BROTHER Big Brother is derived from George Orwell's novel *1984*, a dystopian vision of a society where the invisible state is always watching its inhabitants. The term is better known as the reality television show produced by Dutch company Endemol (an amalgam of its founders, John de Mol and Joop Van den Ende). It first ran in Holland in 1999 and has since become a phenomenon in over seventy countries. There are two versions in the UK (one with celebrities and one without), broadcast in January and August, where up to fifteen contestants are not allowed to leave the confines of a house and, one by one, nominate each other for eviction, which is then determined by phone votes from the public. The last remaining member is declared the winner.

• • •

Celebrity Big Brother 2006 provided the greatest moment in contemporary UK Jewish history when George Galloway, MP for Bethnal Green and Bow, was thrown out of the *Big Brother* house. Mr Galloway, known for his fanatical criticism of Israel and his dogged support of known anti-Semites, was utterly humiliated in the contest after pretending to be a cat in one of the tasks. Kneeling in front of actress Rula Lenska, he purred while lapping her palms in search of imaginary milk. Revenge comes to those who wait, Oona.

Aside from this happy, happy day, there is little for the Judologist to concern him/herself over with this show. Hardly any Jewish contestants have appeared (anti-Semitism or self-preservation?). When they have, they have been dismissed quickly. Witness Justine Sellman, a sales manager from Leeds, who was voted off *Big Brother* 4 in 2003. It is hard to argue the Great British Public was expelling her for her Jewishness, but her love of designer clothes and hair straighteners did not help.

Science, the rapper from *Big Brother* 6, described himself as a Black Jew. He was reported to have said, 'I'm not a part of no Jewish church or stuff like that' (*Totally Jewish*, July 2005). So that makes him clearly a part of one, no? Vanessa Feltz and Caprice both exited early in their appearances on the show, which begs us to believe that the Jewish track record for 'fitting in' runs true to form.

What is the fuss all about? Think about it. Someone

watching your every move, listening to all your conversations (especially about sex), making you feel like everybody's talking about you every minute? Isn't this just normal life for young Jewish children? It should be renamed *Big Jewish Mother* or *Oy, I'm a Jew, Get Me Outta Here*.

---

backlash + impact x j-factor = tzurus ÷ kabbalah = good/not good

3.5   + 6.5   x 5.7   = 57   ÷ 7   = 8.14

☀ ***BIG BROTHER* IS GOOD FOR THE JEWS.**

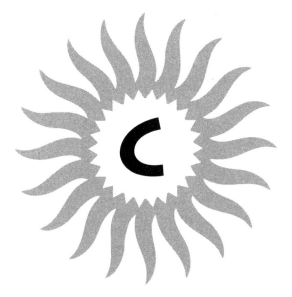

CHEESECAKE A dessert made from cheese, often cream cheese, usually with a biscuity base. There are many different varieties created by adding other ingredients such as nuts, chocolate or fruit, using different types of cheese, using different types of base or cooking for different lengths of time. Cheesecake was served to athletes during the first Olympic Games in 776 BC. The Romans then took cheesecake from Greece to the rest of Europe.

◆　◆　◆

Is there a spiritual quality to cheesecake? It is the dish of the Jewish festival Shavuot, when Jews commemorate the giving of the Ten Commandments to Moses and the Israelites. Why did the starving, overheated Jews want cheesecake, of all things, to celebrate this turning point in their history?

Cheese makes important appearances in the Bible. One of the many names for Mount Sinai in Hebrew is Bar Gavnunim (mountain of peaks) – the same root as 'gevinah', the word for cheese. Some speculate (*The Jewish Journal of Los Angeles*, 2002) that the Israelites had left camp for so long to listen to all the new rules that their milk turned sour and became cheese. Either way, it would make more sense for us to eat cheese balls or cheese soufflé rather than cheesecake, wouldn't it?

Cheese has also been key to fighting. Cheese is mentioned in the Bible (I Samuel 1:17–18) when a young shepherd boy brings some ten cheeses to the battlefield to feed the soldiers who were fighting the mighty Philistines. The young man bringing this important food? David, the slayer of the giant Goliath and Israel's second king.

The role of cheese in defeating Israel's enemies does not end there. Judith defeated Holofernes in the Book of Judith by feeding him salty cheese. The cunning vixen knew that his *fromage*-induced thirst would create a craving for wine (which she happened to have at the ready by the bedside), which made him sleepy, which allowed Judith to chop off his head and save the Jews from this homicidal general in Nebuchadnezzar's army. Cheese and wine parties will never be the same again.

For the lactose-intolerant, and there are many in the Jewish community, cheesecake is torture and should be avoided. It is also so rich that it contributes to heart-attacks.

---

backlash + impact x j-factor = tzurus ÷ kabbalah = good/not good
1.45   + 3.5   x 6.15   = 30.44 ÷ 7   = 4.35

☀ CHEESECAKE IS NOT GOOD FOR THE JEWS.

CHOLERA Originated on the Indian subcontinent. The bacteriologist Robert Koch (1843–1910) identified the *Vibrio cholerae* bacterium that causes this infectious disease. Cholera is passed from human to human by drinking water or eating food contaminated with the bacterium. In an epidemic, the source of the contamination is usually the faeces (stool) of an infected person. In the United States, cholera was prevalent in the 1800s but has been virtually eliminated by modern sewage and water-treatment systems. As with most great pestilences, Jews have been blamed for bringing it to the world. The great Hamburg cholera epidemic of 1892 was blamed on Jews from the East (Ostjuden); in the same year, the Ostjuden were blamed for bringing cholera and typhus to New York, and President Benjamin Harrison halted the flow of immigration into the country. This closed the door to many Jews fleeing the progroms in Russia.

* * *

Tell me, who is cholera good for exactly?

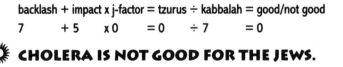

backlash + impact x j-factor = tzurus ÷ kabbalah = good/not good
7   + 5   x 0   = 0   ÷ 7   = 0

CHOLERA IS NOT GOOD FOR THE JEWS.

CHOLESTEROL. Cholesterol is a waxy substance found in the bloodstream and in the body's cells. It is healthy in small amounts. A high level of cholesterol in the blood is a major risk factor for coronary heart disease, which leads to heart-attack. It's also a risk factor for stroke. Hypercholesterolemia is the term for high levels of blood cholesterol. Cholesterol is generated in the body and is found in foods such as fish, meat, eggs, cheese, butter and milk. Food from plants – like fruits, vegetables and cereals – doesn't contain cholesterol.

◆　◆　◆

Cholesterol is not a great friend to the Jewish lover of food. Strudel, cholent, salt beef, cheesecake, chopped liver, all mainstays of the Jewish home, contain low-density lipoprotein (LDL), which clogs up your arteries. 'Feh!' you might say if you are one of the many East European Ashkenazi Jewish centenarians brought up on a rich, high-cholesterol diet. Some recent studies have supported the heredity argument: a variant form has been found of a gene called *CETP*; this gene encodes the cholesterylester transfer protein (CETP), which helps form and move cholesterol particles around the body, and the variant may be linked to longevity. Even better news came when it was reported that some genetic variations benefit a Jewish population and might not occur in other ethnic groups (source: *Science News*, vol. 164).

Does that mean Jews can gorge themselves on tzimmes and potato kugel whilst non-Jews have to become vegetarians? Could this finally be the reason why Jews are the Chosen People?

Unlikely. Remember, Jews are commanded to 'Watch yourselves very carefully' (Deuteronomy 4:15), and, with the BSE and bird flu scares, it might be time for Jews to give up their triple-deck deli sandwiches and, get excited by parsnips and broccoli. Heart disease in particular kills 50 per cent of Britons, and that includes Jewish Britons.

A Jewish breakthrough in the fight against cholesterol came by way of Dr Shela Gorinstein, who helped develop the hybrid fruit called pomelit, which can significantly lower cholesterol levels. Two Jews won the Nobel Prize for their work on regulating cholesterol (Michael S. Brown/Joseph L. Goldstein, 1985). So Jews are not good for cholesterol.

---

backlash + impact x j-factor = tzurus ÷ kabbalah = good/not good
1.5   + 6.4   x 4.8   = 37.9 ÷ 7   = 5.4

 CHOLESTEROL IS NOT GOOD FOR THE JEWS

COLONIC IRRIGATION (ALSO CALLED COLONICS AND COLON HYDROTHERAPY)

A procedure where warm water is pumped into the intestinal tract through a rubber tube that is inserted 20 inches into the patient's backside. Sometimes the water is spiked with special herbs or wheat grass extract or other substances to help the flow. Also known as the 'autointoxication' theory, the practice can be traced back to the ancient Egyptians and led to the popularity of colonic irrigation as a supposed cure.

◆　◆　◆

Marilyn Monroe once confided to her psychiatrist, Dr Ralph Greenson, that Mae West was given an enema every day and said it kept her young. She also recommended one orgasm a day, but that doesn't fit into this entry, as it were.

What does colonic irrigation have to do with the Jews? According to the Bible (and Dr Jerry Glenn Knox, author of *Love Thine Enemas and Heal Thyself*), the colon is the seat of the personality. It is said that constipated people are nervous, irritable and hard to get along with. People with good bowel function tend to be congenial, relaxed and more 'at home with themselves'. Clearly it would be a massive generalization to say Jews are uptight, irritable and nervy, but there has been a sharp rise in colonic therapy within the Jewish community in recent years.

Scientists have argued that a large colon can be inherited and is common among some ethnic groups, such as Ashkenazi Jews. Dr Knox relates the following story of a patient who would go up to 'eleven days between bowel movements . . . She had a massive colon. I believe this is the reason that many Ashkenazis have a syndrome in which they have idiopathic abdominal pain.' In other words, Jews simply don't need to defecate as much as non-Jews, but they sure like to complain about it. Famously, Jack Osbourne, son of Sharon and Ozzy, underwent a week-long, twice-daily regime of colonic irrigation, lost 10 pounds and weaned himself off booze and drugs – an appealing prospect for Jews who wish to let it all hang out and fight off the effects of too much lokshen pudding.

Vichy, in France, is famous for its mud baths and colonic treatments. However, improving the residents' bowel functions did not seem to relax the towns-people's attitude to Jews when they collaborated with Hitler in 1940.

---

backlash + impact x j-factor = tzurus ÷ kabbalah = good/not good
3.0   + 3.3   x 1.5   = 9.45   ÷ 7   = 1.35

 COLONIC IRRIGATION IS NOT GOOD FOR THE JEWS.

COMPLAINING Webster's dictionary defines the verb to complain as 'to express grief, pain or discontent or to make a formal accusation or charge'. *Kvetsch* is the Yiddish word for this term. Woody Allen defined kvetsching with this joke: two old yentas sitting in a restaurant. 'The food here is just awful.' The other agrees, 'Yes, and such small portions.'

◆   ◆   ◆

It is not just anti-Semites who have given the Jews cause to grumble. They manage quite well on their own. One could read the book of Exodus as one long gripe as the Jews escape slavery and wander through the desert to freedom: the food is no good (manna), nobody listens to us (golden calf), this long schlep and *fur wus*? In Egypt, they might have beaten us black and blue and raped our daughters, but at least the trains ran on time, etc. Mind you, forty years, by anyone's standards, is a long time to go property hunting, and their boss did go off for long periods with no word.

All cultures complain. Is campaigning for civil rights complaining? Is marching against the war in Iraq complaining? Is asking for a decent portion instead of this vershimmalte excuse for a brisket of lamb complaining? Is writing endless letters to the *Guardian* about its coverage of Israel complaining? As someone famously said, 'To err is human, to complain divine.' But there is something uniquely Jewish about complaining. For example, two famous stories to show the difference in ethnic complaining.

Grandma Esti is playing with her beloved grandson, Heskell, on the beach when a huge wave comes and snatches him out to sea. '*A klog iz mir!*' she screams. '*Got in himl*, save my little Heskell! I'll do anything – go to shul more, I'll even keep kosher! I beg of you, bring him back.' Suddenly, the rage of the sea quietens and, as if by a miracle, the little boy is delivered to her on the seashore. Grandma Esti looks up to the skies and says, 'And the hat?'

A devout Christian joins a monastery, a new order where the vow of silence is broken only once every seven years, when he is allowed to say two words. After the first seven years, he is summoned to see the Abbot, Augustus, and quietly says his two words: 'Very draughty.' Brother Augustus nods. Seven more years pass. The young man coughs and whispers his words, 'Hard floor.' Brother Augustus nods. Seven more years pass. 'I quit,' he says. Brother Augustus sighs and says, 'Well, that's no surprise, you've done nothing but complain since the moment you got here.'

Perhaps complaining is a survival instinct?

---

backlash + impact x j-factor = tzurus ÷ kabbalah = good/not good
4.25   + 4.35 x 6.85 = 58.91 ÷ 7   = 8.42

☀ **COMPLAINING IS GOOD FOR THE JEWS.**

WORLD TIMELINE
(PART I – FROM THE CREATION TO JESUS)

Here are two brief timelines running concurrently to aid the Judologist who wishes to refresh their memory of past events that were good for the Jews and those that we wish to forget. The author wishes to make it clear that they are not definitive.

WORLD

4.55 billion years BC	150,000 BC	50,000 BC	3760 BC	1875–1445 BC	1444–800 BC	776 BC	600–500 BC	100 BC – AD 100
Earth formed	First signs of homo sapiens	Man arrives in Europe	Jewish calendar begins	Egyptians enslave Israelites	First code of laws	Olympic Games	Babylon destroys Temple (586)	Jesus born and died
					Moses frees Jews		Democracy develops in Athens	Romans destroy Temple (AD 70)
					Solomon builds Temple in Jerusalem			

JEWISH

4.55 billion years BC	150,000 BC	50,000 BC	3760 BC	1875–1445 BC	1445–800 BC	776 BC	600–500 BC	100 BC – AD 100
No, the world was created 5,767 years ago	Nonsense, the world was created 5,767 years ago	Oy ya broch, *the world was created 5,767 years ago*	At last, someone believes me!	Bad job prospects for Jews	First lawyer paid	No interest to Jews	Jerusalem house prices plummet	Our tzurus begins
					Lots of Jews wandering		Jews have more opinions	Tzurus increases
					Jerusalem house prices shoot up			

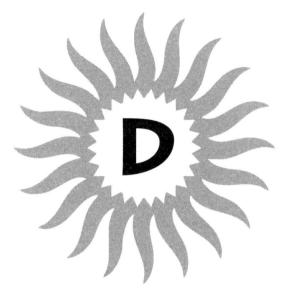

DEEP THROAT (THE MAN) (William Mark Felt, Sr, born 17 August 1913) Felt was second in command at the FBI during the Watergate investigations; he was also the main informant to the *Washington Post* of the link between the Watergate Hotel break-in and the White House. He was known to the newspaper as Deep Throat, so called by reporter Bob Woodward to keep his identity secret. The information he supplied led to the resignation of President Richard M. Nixon in 1974. His identity was finally revealed in 2005 by his family in an article in *Vanity Fair* magazine.

●　　●　　●

Mark Felt is the man who brought down that Republican *mamzer* Nixon. The man surely must be good for the Jews? The fact that Nixon suspected he was Jewish adds a large dose of schadenfreude as well. According to the *Washington Post*, Nixon inquired as to Felt's religion and exclaimed, '[Expletive], [the bureau] put a Jew in there?' To which his chief of staff, Bob Haldeman, responded, 'Well, that could explain it.'

Though Mr Felt is not Jewish – he is of Irish descent and claims no religious affiliation – his Jewish-sounding name might make people *think* he is and blame the Jews for meddling with the FBI and betraying the president. Added to this, Nixon was busy trying to help Israel during its toughest war, the Yom Kippur War in 1973, so one could argue that any distraction from this was not good for the Jews.

Traitor or hero?

Felt's name might sound Jewish, but does he look Jewish? The pictures taken outside his home on the day of the publication of the *Vanity Fair* article made him look more like one of those old Nazi war criminals one finds hanging out in Bolivia than the *shammus* at one's local shul.

---

backlash + impact x j-factor = tzurus ÷ kabbalah = good/not good
6.24   + 4.17 x 2   = 20.82 ÷ 7   = 2.97

☀ DEEP THROAT (THE MAN) IS NOT GOOD FOR THE JEWS.

DEEP THROAT (THE MOVIE)

Released in the summer of 1972, written and directed by Gerard Damiano and starring Linda Lovelace, *Deep Throat* was the first pornographic movie to be shown in mainstream cinemas.

Deep Throat is about a young woman (Linda Lovelace) who discovers that her clitoris is located in her throat; she can only achieve orgasm by 'deep throating' men, thereby achieving contact with her elusively placed genitalia.

♦   ♦   ♦

Harry Reems shot to fame playing the doctor who helps his patient 'come to her senses'. He was the first Hebrew in history to be known for the size of his putz. The outrageous profit made on this skin-flick (it cost $24,000 to make and grossed $600 million) was rumoured to have been pocketed by Colombian mob lords, but there was very little involvement from Jews in the making and distribution of this movie. In the documentary on the film (*Inside Deep Throat*, 2005), virtually all of the contributors are Jewish (Annie Sprinkle, Al Goldstein, Alan Dershowitz, Dr Ruth Westheimer), which gives the impression that the movie was a Jewish event. This is patently untrue. After all, which Jewish movie would wax lyrical about an act unperformed in any Jewish household? On the other hand, as a wish fulfilment fantasy, *Deep Throat* scores high for being good for Jews.

However, one can see the movie as a treatise on disability – for what else is a clitoris in your throat other than a physical impairment? – and as such is neither good nor bad for the Jews. In 2005, a Swedish study by Kerstin Rosenquist at Malmö University found a link between oral sex and mouth cancer. Proof, finally, that Mother knows best.

---

backlash + impact x j-factor = tzurus ÷ kabbalah = good/not good
4.5   + 4.25 x 5.75   = 50.31 ÷ 7   = 7.18

☀ *DEEP THROAT,* THE MOVIE, IS BORDER-LINE AND THEREFORE NOT GOOD FOR THE JEWS.

DESPERATE HOUSEWIVES Channel Four's *Desperate Housewives* is described as 'a primetime soap with a truly contemporary take on "happily every after", [which] takes a darkly comedic look at suburbia, where the secret lives of housewives aren't always what they seem'(source: ABC website). It is narrated from the grave by the character Mary Alice, who committed suicide at the start of the first series, which aired in October 2001. She tells the stories of the friends and family she left behind on Wisteria Lane, and reveals the very dark undercurrent that runs beneath the surface of picture-perfect suburban life.

Desperate Housewives stars Teri Hatcher, Felicity Huffman, Marcia Cross, Eva Longoria, Nicollette Sheridan, and was created by Marc Cherry.

•   •   •

Without a single Jewish character or plotline, *Desperate Housewives* must be seen as a minimal threat to the Jews. However, most of the production team and writers are Jewish, and the concept of a 'desperate housewife' was identified by a Jewish feminist, Betty

Friedan, in her classic book, *The Feminine Mystique*. Also, Eva Longoria (Gabrielle Solis) did make her theatrical debut in *What the Rabbi Saw*.

Some have been angered by the show's moral ambiguity. A furore was kicked up in the States when ABC, the US television network that created the show, ended its Easter Sunday tradition of airing the classic 1956 film *The Ten Commandments* so that *Desperate Housewives* could run in primetime. Shunting off the great biblical epic which shows the Jews defeating the Egyptians was, undoubtedly, a highly controversial act of aggression. The Easter 2005 episode was the most watched programme in the USA – more than 24 million people tuned in. Perhaps to this MTV generation the sight of Moses smashing the tablets while the Israelites worship the Golden Calf cannot compete with the sight of Lynette swallowing pills while Gabrielle humps the gardener? Tough, but sometimes religion has to take a back seat.

Plans were announced in September 2005 to dub the series into Spanish for the potential 11 million Hispanic viewers in the USA. The Yiddish version is still under discussion, with Channel Four executives favouring the title *Shtupping Shiksas*.

---

backlash + impact x j-factor = tzurus ÷ kabbalah = good/not good
3.45   + 5.05   x 3.24   = 27.54 ÷ 7   = 3.93

✹ *DESPERATE HOUSEWIVES* IS NOT GOOD FOR THE JEWS.

DISNEY, WALT A cartoonist who won fame and fortune in the entertainment industry through his films, television series and theme parks. Born on 5 December 1901 in Chicago, Illinois and interested in drawing from a young age, he went to Hollywood in 1923. With his brother Roy as business manager, he opened a new studio and produced a series of cartoons featuring a character called Oswald the Rabbit. When sound was introduced to film in 1927, Walt invented Mickey Mouse and provided the character's voice himself. By 1966, the year of his death, he had made some of the most successful children's movies of all time: *Bambi*, *Mary Poppins*, *Snow White and the Seven Dwarfs*, *Fantasia*, *The Jungle Book* and *Dumbo*, to name but a few. In 1955 he also opened his first theme park, Disneyland Park. Disney theme parks now include Disneyland, Walt Disney World, Euro Disney and Tokyo Disney. Walt's nephew, Roy Disney, led a shareholders' revolt against CEO Michael Eisner in 2003 and 2004. As a result Eisner relinquished his position as CEO in 2004 and stepped down as chairman in 2005. In 2006 Pixar was acquired by Disney for $4.1 billion. The deal made Steve Jobs, founder of Apple, the biggest single shareholder of the company.

●   ◆   ●

There are theories that Mickey Mouse is Jewish, and that this explained Hitler's antipathy to the big-eared rodent, but there is no evidence to support this, despite the huge sales in Mickey Mouse mezzuzahs and menorahs in the early nineties. Mind you, he does have a bossy wife called Minnie . . .

Walt himself was supposedly not too keen on Jews. He reportedly refused to employ Jews in high-level positions at his studio or as actors in his live-action features. Only after his death did a Jewish actor feature prominently in a Disney film (Buddy Hackett in *The Love Bug*, 1969). It might be argued that some of the messages in the films were not exactly conducive to harmonious race relations. Let's face it, *The Jungle Book* had the king of swing, Louis Prima, voice the monkey; Dumbo is taunted by black crows who sing da blues, one of which is actually called Jim Crow; and Pinocchio is a boy who wears a skullcap and whose nose grows as a result of lying. I don't know . . . do I smell a theme?

Ironic, then, that Disney became a worldwide superbrand between 1984 and 2005 under a Jew, Michael Eisner. Southern Baptists and many family organizations attempted boycotts after hearing of Eisner's plans for a Gay Day and after Ellen Degeneres came out on her Disney-made show, *Ellen*. The final nail in the coffin occurred when he bought Miramax, the company that produced *Reservoir Dogs* and other ungodly movies, formerly owned by the Weinstein brothers. Some writers have seen this 'judification' of the great institution of Disney as 'another instrument

in the Jewish campaign to multiculturalize America'
(William L. Pierce, *Disney and the Jews: Eisner and His
Kind Must Stop Harming Our Children*).

Shrek (Yiddish expression of terror) released by
Dreamworks in 2001, would have had ole Walt turning
in his grave. Not only did it outgross *Toy Story*, the pio-
neering Disney/Pixar blockbuster, but it mercilessly sent
up Disney's hold on our favourite fairytale characters.
Disney's response to this alien onslaught? *Pocahontas II*.

Things have picked up since those turbulent days.
The first of seven *Chronicles of Narnia* was launched in
December 2005 and grossed $209,119,000 (as of
3 January 2006; source: movieweb.com). The film's
subtle Christian allusions were not lost on the
Christian groups that adopted it with a fervour and a
frenzy last seen during the *Passion of the Christ* marketing
campaign. Sadly, Aslan was not mutilated and tortured
for two hours, thus making it a fully fledged Christian
movie, but Walden Media (the co-producer, whose
owner is a Republican Christian devoted to spreading
the word of Narnia to every schoolchild in the nation)
was happy to steer Disney back from the abyss with
this wholesome all-round American entertainment.

---

backlash + impact x j-factor = tzurus ÷ kabbalah = good/not good
6.1   + 7   x 4.25 = 55.67 ÷ 7   = 7.95

 **WALT DISNEY IS BORDERLINE AND
THEREFORE NOT GOOD FOR THE JEWS.**

EASTENDERS Launched on 19 February 1985, BBC1's highest-rating soap is set in the fictional community of Walford, east London. The East End is a popular term for the area traditionally defined as the districts to the east of the City of London which covers the boroughs of Stepney, Bethnal Green, Shoreditch, Poplar, Tower Hamlets and parts of Hackney.

•   •   •

How can the East End have no Jewish characters? This area has always been dominated by ethnic communities – the Jews, Bangladeshis, Pakistanis, Huguenots, Gudjeratis – yet this is not reflected in the most popular serial on the BBC. Judologists must carefully examine the evidence.

The argument for *EastEnders* not having Jews in the storylines goes as follows:

1) Michael Grade commissioned it and probably didn't want to come over as 'too Jewish'.
2) The Jews have moved out of the East End and now inhabit the leafy suburbs of north London. Unless episodes are filled with heritage tours around abandoned

    Sephardi synagogues on the Mile End Road, it is unlikely there will be much Jewish background content in future storylines.

3) Jews are so assimilated in this country nobody knows what a Jew is.

The argument against *EastEnders* having no Jews in the storylines goes as follows:

1) When they tried it, it was boring – think Doctor Legg, Rachel Kominsky, Felix the barber, Vince Watson and Nigel's girlfriend's son. If Jews are this dull, keep them off primetime.

2) Every time the BBC has tried putting Jews on telly they have resulted in horrendous stereotypes: *Agony* (remember the Jewish mother Bea? Agony is not the word), *So Haunt Me* (which still does) and Dorian in *Birds of a Feather* (a Jewish Joan Collins) – so perhaps it is time to let go and not be represented in mainstream British broadcasting.

The most prominent Jewish actor in the series is Tracy-Ann Obermann, who looks Jewish to everyone but the population of Norfolk and Yorkshire, who have never seen a Jew before.

However, don't think that the fact that the character is called Chrissie Watts means Ms Obermann won't be registering high on every Jewish household's J-dar. Let's hope the fact the character is a murderous, scheming vixen bent on taking over the family business has nothing to do with her casting.

Although the East End of London provided refuge for fleeing refugees, and Jewish life thrived relatively unchallenged (Cable Street Riots aside), most Jews are relieved to have left the poverty and the smell of gefilte fish behind them. However, most Jews now wish they had kept a small studio flat there – have you seen the prices now in that schmutzigge Hoxton?

---

backlash + impact x j-factor = tzurus ÷ kabbalah = good/not good
3.5   + 2.5   x 1.5   = 9   ÷ 7   = 1.28

✳ *EASTENDERS* IS NOT GOOD FOR THE JEWS.

EASTER. A Christian festival celebrating the resurrection of Jesus after the crucifixion. Easter marks the end of the forty days of Lent, a period of fasting and penitence, which begins on Ash Wednesday and ends on Easter Sunday.

•   ◆   •

Historically, not the best time of year for Jews. The only show in town is the Passion Play, which tends to depict Jews as treacherous murderers. Traditionally it has been a time for Jews to lie low as feelings can rise high, especially in parts of Eastern Europe, Venezuela and the whole of East Anglia. Because Easter falls around Passover time, a further wave of hostility emerged with the Blood Libel – the accusation that Jews were using the blood of Christian children to make matzoh. However, this recipe does not appear in the classic *Book of Jewish Food* by Claudia Roden (Viking, 1996).

All in all, Easter for Jews is like Christmas for turkeys, or grouse season for, well, grouse. It is a time to pretend you don't exist. Is there any upside to this season? Jews get to buy bulkloads of Easter eggs at massively reduced prices after the three-day fest is over. In fact, chocoholic Muslims, Hindus and Jews can be seen working together in picking over the spoils at the 'highly discounted' sections of Woolworths on the Tuesday following Easter. And all for Christian-themed sweets. Thus, Easter can be a time to bring religions and races together.

One could see the coincidence of Passover and Easter falling at the same time of year as a sign. The Last Supper was, after all, a seder; Jesus is seen as the Paschal Lamb; in most languages Easter is called Pasch ('Easter', unsurprisingly comes from a pagan goddess); and both festivals close with a huge sigh of relief as the gluttony and close proximity to family members finally come to an end.

---

backlash + impact x j-factor = tzurus ÷ kabbalah = good/not good

$7 \quad + 6.8 \quad x\ 3.35 \quad = 46.23 \div 7 \quad\quad = 6.60$

☀ **EASTER IS NOT GOOD FOR THE JEWS.**

EBAY Online auction site where people can buy and sell almost anything from or to anyone anywhere in the world. It was started in 1995 by Pierre Omidyar and its name is a rather tasteless nod to the efficacy of the Ebola virus. It now claims to be one of the fastest-growing companies of all time. Transactions are based on good faith between the buyer and seller. eBay displays feedback from buyers and sellers to encourage honesty.

❖   ❖   ❖

Where else can the acquisitive Judologist buy a Harvey Megillah dancing Hasid doll? Mind you, up until May 2001, you could also buy Hitler's pencil case and nasal trimmer, so free markets do have their downsides. eBay did cave in to pressure from the Anti-Defamation League over making profits from Nazi memorabilia and now bans material associated with murders committed in the past 100 years (except stamps and coins and WWII movies, etc.), so you can still buy *Schindler's List*.

One can still buy some great items of anti-Semitic interest. Hundreds of copies of the *Protocols of the Elders of Zion*, *Mein Kampf* and other good old-fashioned race-hate products can be snapped up at a bargain. Strangely, for a dotcom business, the founder of this celebration of free enterprise is neither Jewish (jewwatch.com better change its 'educational website') nor American born, but French Iranian. Mr Omidyar has used his fortune in a heimische way, though, and set up charitable foundations with his wife that pour millions into public projects.

But what to do if your auction date is set for Shabbos or, even worse, Rosh Hashanah? As everybody knows, the last moments of an eBay auction matter the most. Could this be a coded anti-Semitic way of excluding Jews from top products? Imagine the sheer vindictiveness of a deadline of Kol Nidre night on the eve of Yom Kippur for, say, the complete *Seinfeld* backlist or, worse, a tallis in pristine condition worn by the Lubavitcher Rebbe? Torture.

---

backlash + impact x j-factor = tzurus ÷ kabbalah = good/not good
4.5   + 6.45   x 4.1   = 44.89 ÷ 7   = 6.41

☀ EBAY IS NOT GOOD FOR THE JEWS.

EUROVISION SONG CONTEST Inspired by the popular Italian San Remo Festival, the Eurovision Song Contest was first held in Lugano, Switzerland in 1956 and was billed as *The Eurovision Grand Prix*. The winner was chosen by a jury consisting of two delegates from each country. Though widely ridiculed for the poor quality of performances and anachronistic national costumes, it is hugely popular in Europe, the Middle East and Africa and is a mainstay of light-entertainment live broadcasting. Conventionally, the host nation is determined by the winner of the previous year's contest. Many international artists have competed in the ESC. These include Celine Dion, Olivia Newton-John and Abba.

◆　◆　◆

Jews everywhere take serious note of this competition, not necessarily because of their appreciation of the art of the pop song, but because it provides a good gauge of international feelings towards the Jews.

The elaborate voting system involves each nation assigning points to its favourite ten entries. Until recently votes were decided by small juries in each country; now national telephone polls are held during the live broadcast in order to determine points assignment. Countries are not allowed to vote for themselves.

Hence the Jewish obsession with this competition. Ever since Israel joined the competition in 1973, oohs and ahs and I told you sos can be heard in households throughout Europe when Lithuania, Austria or Poland cast their negative votes for Israel. Other countries suffer too. The UK's 2003 act Jemini did not receive a single point from any European country, which was interpreted as an expression of anger at the war in Iraq. Cyprus and Greece always give each other maximum points regardless of the dreck offered up. They never vote for Turkey.

Israel being part of Europe might be news to most people, but since they have won three times, we should let this drop. These Jewish heroes were: Alpha Beta (1978); Milk and Honey (geddit?) (1979); transvestite and gay icon Dana International (1998).

Some might argue that the mighty Israel, feared in the Middle East, might not be best represented by a man who wears dresses and a group of terrible perms. However, to be invited to any party these days is a metziah.

YES, BUT IS IT GOOD FOR THE JEWS?

backlash + impact x j-factor = tzurus ÷ kabbalah = good/not good
5.45   + 5.56 x 5.45   = 60   ÷ 7   = 8.57

 THE EUROVISION SONG CONTEST IS GOOD FOR THE JEWS.

F

FOX NEWS CHANNEL, THE Owned by Rupert Murdoch's News International Corporation, the channel, launched in 1996, was set up to rival CNN and soon began taking its market share of audience. Murdoch, known for his opposition to what he believed was a liberal agenda in the media, was determined to take an alternative editorial stance in his network. Initially shut out of the New York market by Time Warner, CNN's parent company, Fox News was made available there in 1997 and on the rest of Time Warner's vast cable network in 2001.

❖ ❖ ❖

Fox CEO Roger Ailes was a former strategist for Nixon and Reagan, so balanced reporting is his watchword. Fox News saw its profits double during the Iraq War, and some say this is due to its patriotic (i.e. pro-war) coverage. At the height of the conflict, it had 3.3 million viewers daily.

One of Fox News' many slogans is 'Fair and Balanced'. An example of this approach, according to bangitout.com, came in the form of a report from Jerusalem, filed by the intrepid reporter Geraldo Riviera. When asked by Greta Van Susteran what the mood was like in downtown Jerusalem, he responded, 'People are not hopeful, Greta. Hope is not here. There is no hope.' He went on to describe deserted streets and empty cafés, but his balance began to waver when he proclaimed that the sky was devoid of hope, as well: 'No, not in the sky, either. No hope in the sky. I looked, and it is not there'. Perhaps some reporters at Fox double as meteorologists? He ended his sober report with: 'Life is not the same. Here in Israel. Here. In. Israel. This has been Geraldo Riviera, reporting live and trying not to cry.' Fairly balanced reporting at its best.

The challenge might be for the Judologist to find anything *bad* for the Jews in Fox News. Famously, it dropped the term 'suicide bomber' and replaced it, upon the request of Ari Fleischer, President Bush's Press Secretary, with 'homicide bomber'. Fairness and Accuracy in Reporting (FAIR) released a report entitled *The Most Biased Name in News: Fox News Channel's Right-Wing Tilt.*

Of course, Fox is not just a fanatical right-wing mouthpiece for the Bush administration. It is much more extreme than that. However, to be 'fair and balanced', one should recognize Roger Ailes' very proud scoop on Bush's hidden drink-driving offence before the 2000 presidential election. This, according to Karl Rove, 'cost Bush the popular vote'. Does he mean that Bush won the 'unpopular vote'?

Just so Jews don't feel too comfortable with Fox News' attitudes, remember Bill O'Reilly, the channel's

most obvious exponent of 'We Report, You Decide'
values, said about Christmas,

You have a predominantly Christian nation. You have a federal holiday based on the philosopher Jesus. And you don't
wanna hear about it? Come on – if you are really offended,
you gotta go to Israel, then. I mean, because we live in a
country founded on Judeo- – and that's your guys' –
Christian – that's my guys' – philosophy. But overwhelm-
ingly, America is Christian. And the holiday is a federal
holiday honouring the philosopher Jesus.

How Fox News would have covered the following news
stories had it been around 2000 years ago:

Billionaire's Twin Betrayal

Brotherly love seemed to be in short supply in Canaan this
evening, when our Fox News correspondent, Frank Ramos,
caught up with a developing story that has rocked the small
town of Elon. A sting operation, more commonly seen practised in downtown Little Moab, is alleged to have occurred in
the early hours of Sunday morning.

Esau, 34, is heir to the Isaac Forefather billion-shekel fortune. Although a twin, he is older than his brother, Jacob
Isaacson, and therefore expected to receive his birthright and
father's blessing, both of which are compulsory under the
new heredity laws.

That was until Jacob, sensationally, dressed in his

brother's clothes in order to trick his ailing father into giving him his brother's rightful blessing. Allegations of blackmail have been made by Esau after papers were submitted to the town hall transferring his birthright to Jacob one year prior to today's shocking events. 'Technically, there is nothing we can do,' the DA of Canaan County confirms. 'Unless the young man returns the birthright on his own volition, I'm afraid it looks like Esau will have to accept this loophole in the Law.'

Jacob has left town, and his mother, Rebekka (aged 108), is helping local police with their inquiries. Local reports are coming in of a wandering homeless man who fits Jacob's description, picked up on the road to Luza, but this is yet to be confirmed.

New Legislation Threatens Small Business

Copies of the 613 new regulations introduced since the second publication of the Laws of Moses have sent the markets into freefall, Milton Simkins, our financial correspondent, reports.

The SHMTSE fell by a record 299 points, its steepest one-day decline since the Israelites left Egypt. Laws which will go into force in April next year are set to revolutionize the meat, fish and poultry sectors, as well as completely overhaul the existing regulations governing the textile and fashion industries.

'I have to slaughter the animals in totally different ways now,' Shlomo Anov, the spokesperson for the Abbatoir Union said. 'New knives, new salting procedures, new everything. These statutes will spell the end to small corner shops.'

'It simply doesn't make sense,' Abe Simcha of the Natural Wool Association says. 'I am now not allowed to mix wool with cotton. There are pages and pages of nonsensical guidelines which give no rhyme or reason to the manufacturer. This will be a disaster.'

A Government spokesman was unavailable for comment.

---

backlash + impact x j-factor = tzurus ÷ kabbalah = good/not good
6.4   + 6.4   x 6.4   = 81.9 ÷ 7   = 11.7

FOX NEWS CHANNEL IS GOOD FOR THE JEWS.

GODFATHER TRILOGY, THE Three films about a fictitious Italian Mafia family. The first one, based on Mario Puzo's 1969 novel *The Godfather* and bearing the same title, was released in 1972. It spawned two sequels: *The Godfather Part II* (1974) and *The Godfather Part III* (1990). All three were directed by Francis Ford Coppola.

'The Godfather' (in Italian, *Padrino*) is a term used to identify the boss of a mafia clan, the eldest or the most representative member of a family. Don Vito's surname, Corleone, recalls the town of Corleone, Sicily.

♦   ♦   ♦

The story of an Italian family and its assimilation within corporate America bears no obvious or direct relevance to the Jews. It has a low Jew count, but significantly, in *Godfather II*, Michael Corleone betrays Hyman Roth, an overtly Jewish character, when the young Godfather attempts to expand into Cuba from Florida. Aside from the wheezing, emphysematic portrayal of this powerful Jew, it cannot be said that this is either a positive or negative depiction of the Jews. The other Jewish character – who's never referred to as Jewish directly – is Moe

Greene (the Bugsy Segal character). In his novel *The Godfathers: The Lost Years*, Mark Winegardner introduces Don Forlenza, whose nickname, the 'Jewish Don', comes because he surrounds himself with Jewish associates.

Although many mobsters were Jewish, the most successful movie of the 1970s deflected attention from the Jews to the Italians, and subsequent representations in mass culture, such as *The Sopranos*, *Goodfellas*, *Analyse This*, have all put the blame for the scourge of organized crime firmly on the shoulders of the Italians. Otherwise, we might well have been subjected to series entitled *The Schneiders*, *Machers* and *Analysis/ Shmanalysis*.

---

backlash + impact x j-factor = tzurus ÷ kabbalah = good/not good
5   + 6.15 x 5.4   = 60.2 ÷ 7   = 8.6

✳ THE *GODFATHER* TRILOGY IS GOOD FOR THE JEWS.

GOOGLE Internet search engine founded in 1998 by Sergey Brin and Larry Page at Stanford University. Initially, Google got 10,000 queries per day, compared with 200 million per day currently. The name 'Google' is a play on the word *googol*, the number represented by 1 followed by 100 zeros.

•   •   •

Both Sergey and Larry, the co-founders of Google, are Jewish, a fact which will either fuel conspiracy theories or make them the most eligible 'nice Jewish boys' on the planet. Larry seems to have put the eek into geek as he made a working printer out of Lego. Yes, LEGO.

Google lists three to four thousand hate sites worldwide, and recent controversy over jewwatch.com proves that having Jewish founders does not stop anti-Semitism on the web. More worrying, though, is the recent fad of self-diagnosis: googling your health symptoms has been proven to cause anxiety and trauma. This is clearly a problem for the Jews. 'Don't Be Evil' is a lovely company motto (disconcertingly an anagram of 'Bend to live', something the company managed to do with its ethics when it came to censoring sites for the Chinese government in 2006), but let's face it, with this much money in such young hands, 'evil is whatever Sergey says is evil' (Eric Schmidt, Google chief executive). Besides, moral statements bear little weight when a Googler is free to make a bomb, construct chemical weapons and learn how to lynch local ethnic minorities, all at the stroke of a keyboard.

However, without Google, this book and many others of its ilk would simply not have been written.

Talks between the Judological Institute of Spiritual Mathematics (JISM) and Google began in 2006 to launch a Jew-only search engine called Joogle, the first all-encompassing directory which filters out all irrelevant information (anything non-Jewish) for the Judologist. Thus far this has stalled due to a lack of interest from Google.

---

backlash + impact x j-factor = tzurus ÷ kabbalah = good/not good
6.8   + 6.9   x 7   = 95.9 ÷ 7   = 13.7

☀ GOOGLE IS GOOD FOR THE JEWS.

GRAPHS

Note to Judologists: a random sample of entries has been plotted on these two graphs. The patterns of dashed lines are purely coincidental.

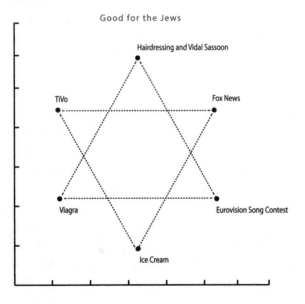

Good for the Jews

Hairdressing and Vidal Sassoon

TiVo   Fox News

Viagra   Eurovision Song Contest

Ice Cream

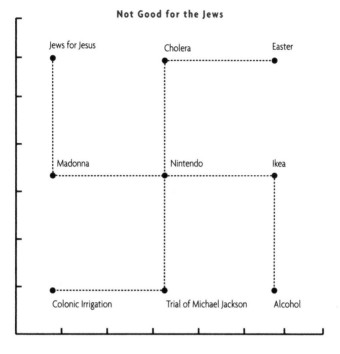

Not Good for the Jews

GUILT Culpability for a crime is the most accepted definition of this term. It also denotes remorseful awareness of having done something wrong or self-reproach for supposed inadequacy or wrongdoing.

◆   ◆   ◆

If you are one of the Chosen People, of course you are going to feel guilty every day of your life about every single aspect of it. After all, you weren't *chosen* to do badly at school, you weren't *chosen* for being unable to finish those gedempte meatballs lovingly cooked by

79

your mother, you weren't *chosen* for your love of being spanked by a Croat animal trainer on Motze Shabbos, and so on. When standards are high, not reaching them can be a cause of guilt.

What happens to the Jew who feels no guilt? Take away the neuroses and remorse for every act performed daily, what are you left with? A non-Jew.

Leviticus had the right idea. Pages and pages of descriptions of how to beat a goat, skin a cat and generally torture the animal world to purge yourself of guilt. Now the Jews don't have scapegoats any more, every malevolent thought is internalized. Mix this with a strong dose of history and you have Jewish guilt.

Guilt expresses itself in countless ways. From the heavy-handed – 'If you don't finish your latkes, Benjamin, your mother and grandmother will drop dead' – to the more subtle approach exemplified by the following story.

During a break in the secret negotiations at Camp David between Israel and Egypt in 1978, Zbigniew Brzezinski, national security adviser to President Jimmy Carter, invited Prime Minister Menachem Begin to play a friendly game of chess with him. Before Mr Brzezinski was allowed to make his first move, Premier Begin dramatically seized his hand in mid-air and said very quietly, 'Dr Brzezinski, do you know when I played my last game of chess?' 'No,' the adviser quivered. 'September 1940, when the NKVD broke into my hiding place in Vilna to arrest me.' Shortly afterwards, Mrs Begin passed. 'Oh, the two of you are playing chess,' she said. 'You know, Mr Brzezinski, Menachem just loves to play. He plays all the time.' (Source: *The Fifty Years War: Israel and the Arabs*, BBC/Norma Percy.)

Without guilt, would peace ever be struck?

---

backlash + impact x j-factor = tzurus ÷ kabbalah = good/not good

5.25   + 5.87 x 7   = 77.84 ÷ 7   = 11.12

☀ **GUILT IS GOOD FOR THE JEWS.**

WORLD TIMELINE
(PART 2 – 1 TO 1000)

WORLD

	1–249	250–500	500–800	500–800	500–800	500–800	850–900	1066
	Gospels are written	Constantine the Great legalizes Christianity (313)	King Arthur legend	Pope Gregory creates 'God Bless You' as the correct response to a sneeze		Arabs conquer Jerusalem	Alfred the Great becomes king of Britain	Norman conquest of Britain
	Goths invade Asia Minor	Attila the Hun invades Roman provinces (433)	Mohammed founds Islam			Russian nation founded by Vikings with capital at Novgorod (855–79)		
	Romans persecute Christians	The Vandals sack Rome (455)	Plague wipes out half of Europe			Muslim invaders destroy Alexandria Library		
						Dome of the Rock built		

JEWISH

	1–249	250–500	500–800	500–800	500–800	500–800	850–900	1066
	Luke outsells Leviticus	Lion-keeping goes underground	*Camelot* opens on Broadway	'Geh, gesundheit' is the street version		Time to sell up again	Who cares?	French move in
	First sign of German trouble	Jews ain't got no quarrel with Asians	I'm not saying anything			First shtetl prepared		
	Jews keep their heads down	You thought Romans were bad	The other half survives			Massive relief to overdue borrowers		
						Ariel Sharon makes first visit		

HAIRDRESSING AND VIDAL SASSOON A world-famous hairdresser and entrepreneur, born in London 17 January 1928, Sassoon rose from humble beginnings to become the father of modern hairdressing. He is the inventor of the bob, the five-point cut and the geometric hairdos perfected during London's swinging sixties. He gave his name to numerous hair products and set up styling academies throughout the UK and US. In 1982, he established the Vidal Sassoon International Center for the Study of Antisemitism. The Center 'engages in research on anti-Semitism throughout the ages, focusing on relations between Jews and non-Jews, particularly in situations of tension and crisis'.

✦   ✦   ✦

Is hairdressing really a profession for a nice Jewish boy? The most famous proponent of this noble art must be Vidal Sassoon. Though famous for his 'Nancy Kwan' cut, he was no nancy boy. Sassoon might have curled and crêped by day, but by night he was rumoured to have been part of a post-war Jewish vigilante group called the 43 Group that hunted out escaped Nazis. In 1948, he left for Israel to help fight in the War of Independence (May 1948). Perhaps his finest moment, though, came when he represented the Jewish people (actually Los Angeles, the host city) in 1984 as Official Hair Stylist at the '84 Olympics, disproving the vicious stereotype that Jews are no good at sporting events.

However, controversy arises when we look at Mr Sassoon's legacy as Hairdresser to the Nation. Young Jewesses everywhere were influenced by him to forego their heimische curls and adopt his geometric cuts and straight hair. The Twiggy and Mia Farrow look plunged Jewish identity into crisis and put a generation of Jewish princesses into therapy for years to come.

The Vidal Sassoon International Center for the Study of Antisemitism spawned many other sober institutions of learning, such as the L'Oréal Because I'm Worth It Research Laboratory for International Peace Studies based in Darlington and, most famously, The Head-and-Shoulders Centre of Islamic Revolution based in Yeovil.

---

backlash + impact x j-factor = tzurus ÷ kabbalah = good/not good

4.5   + 4.0   x 7   = 59.5 ÷ 7   = 8.5

☀ HAIRDRESSING AND VIDAL SASSOON ARE GOOD FOR THE JEWS.

HAPPINESS The state of feeling, showing or causing pleasure or satisfaction. A sense of well-being characterized by emotions ranging from contentment to intense joy.

◆   ◆   ◆

The pursuit of happiness is enshrined as a basic right in the American Declaration of Independence, but for Jews who have experienced so much unhappiness throughout history, is it a surprise that it is not high on the agenda of realistic goals? The consensus among psychologists is that negative emotions are fundamental to the human condition, and the brain works by looking for what's wrong – a response programmed from traumas that go back to the Ice Age. In other words, misery was a state of being that existed before the Jews. Hence the Jews do not have a monopoly on discontent – merely a major stake.

'Man hands on misery to man,' 'Hell is other people,' 'I never knew what happiness really was until I got married. And then it was too late.' These famous quotations are strangely not from Jews but from poet Philip Larkin and the French philosopher Jean-Paul Sartre (non-Jews) and a book of bad jokes. Misery is not a Jewish phenomenon.

Unhappiness is easier to quantify and market than contentment. Psychologists have always preferred the neurotic, the hysteric and the depressed to the happy clappy.

However, a Jewish professor of psychology called Martin Seligman in his bestselling book *Authentic Happiness* scientifically explains what happiness is and how to achieve it. If this works, quite frankly, it could spell disaster for Jewish identity for ever and put a lot of half-decent Jewish comedians out of business.

Seligman maintains you can train your brain to

counter the negative forces. He hates Freud, who he believes harps on about the past and therefore makes you passive about your future. Seligman's formula for happiness includes, among other things: writing down three things that went well every day for a week; identifying your strengths and using one of them in a new and different way every day for a week; writing a letter to someone you're grateful to but have never thanked and go to them and read it out to them.

No wonder we're all so miserable. The stress of finding something good that has happened today would be enough to finish most Jews off.

---

backlash + impact x j-factor = tzurus ÷ kabbalah = good/not good

3.06 + 5.7 x 1.6 = 14.0 ÷ 7 = 2.0

☀ **HAPPINESS IS NOT GOOD FOR THE JEWS.**

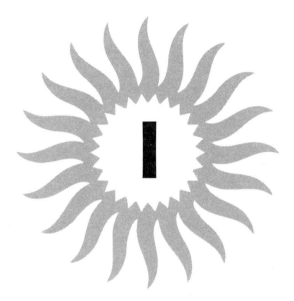

ICE CREAM A frozen dessert made from dairy products, flavourings and sweetners. A cold, pudding-like form of ice cream appeared in Persia in 400 BC. In the thirteenth century the Venetian traveller Marco Polo supposedly saw ice cream being made on his trip to China and brought the recipe home with him on his return. From there, Catherine de Medicis' Italian chefs are said to have carried the recipe to France when she went there in 1533 to marry the Duc d'Orléans. (Source: wikipedia.org.)

✦   ✦   ✦

The Jews cannot be said to have invented ice cream, but the following founders of Forbes 500 companies must take credit for its mass popularity: Rose and Reuben Mattus (Häagen-Dazs), Ben Cohen and Jerry Greenfield (Ben & Jerry), Burton Baskin and Irving Robbins (Baskin-Robbins), Charles Lubin (Sara Lee).

King Solomon the Wise is said to have enjoyed iced drinks during harvest time and he was pretty clever.

---

backlash + impact x j-factor = tzurus ÷ kabbalah = good/not good
4.23   + 6.89 x 5.29 = 58.8 ÷ 7   = 8.4

 ICE CREAM IS GOOD FOR THE JEWS.

IKEA Swedish furniture company created by Ingvar Kamprad in a southern Swedish backwater in 1943. It started as a small business selling matches before diversifying into pencils. Furniture was introduced in 1953. It now has 225 stores in 33 different countries worldwide with a turnover of 14.5 billion Euros. It aims to 'offer a wide range of home furnishings with good design and function at prices so low that as many people as possible will be able to afford them. And still have money left!' (IKEA.com). In some countries the demand for its products is so high that riots have been known to break out when a new store opens, as happened in Edmonton, London in February 2005, at midnight, when over 6,000 customers fought to get in, many sustaining injuries as a result.

IKEA is also a phenomenon in Israel, where, in 2001, it opened one of its biggest stores in the Middle East (23,000 square feet) in Netanya.

◆　◆　◆

What is this mishegoss with do-it-yourself furniture? Cheap it may be, but that is no reason to build it yourself. Whatever happened to the old Jewish maxim 'I'll get a man in'? Jews who are used to building their own sukkahs (tabernacles) might have a leaning towards these products (see SnapSukkah, the do-it-yourself Sukkah), but can IKEA be good for the Jews?

IKEA assembly can be a symbol of Jewish learning, according to one rabbi. 'They always tell you not to tighten the bolts,' explains Tzvi Freeman of the

Chabad organization, 'until the whole thing's been put together.' So it is with Jewish learning: don't expect to know everything until you have learned all the bits and pieces. This, of course, could be just another spurious argument woven by rabbis to get Jews to attend synagogue more.

That aside, it is hard to argue that IKEA is a spiritual experience or one that has been tailored to Jewish needs. Perhaps given IKEA's omnipresence, subliminal messaging might be its more sinister *raison d'être*. After all, with the circulation of its catalogue outstripping that of the Bible (Christian bibles printed in 2003: 53 million; IKEA catalogues printed in 2003: 115 million), could there be a subconscious agenda being transmitted to us via this vast distribution network? A code, perhaps? Is there any Kabbalistic significance to products with names like Bubbla picture holder, Bygel kitchen range, Benjamin stool and Alikvot lamp?

As anyone who has visited an IKEA superstore knows, there is only one direction of traffic allowed and no purchases can be made until the hapless visitor seeking out his plug or one light bulb has reached the checkout at the end of the path through the store. Such power is given over willingly, but to whom? Well, it was rumoured that the founder, Ingvar Kamprad, was once a Nazi, though this charge was subsequently downgraded to mere fascist, which has been massaged to mean 'attending one or two lectures by a minor right-winger called Per

Egndal in Malmö, Sweden in the fifties'. However, in December 1995, Kamprad publicly repented for his flirtation with fascism.

---

backlash + impact x j-factor = tzurus ÷ kabbalah = good/not good
5.03   + 6.67 x 2.2   = 25.74 ÷ 7   = 3.68

✸ IKEA IS NOT GOOD FOR THE JEWS.

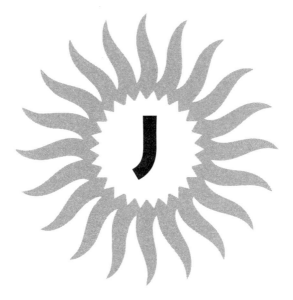

JEANS Jeans were invented in Genoa, Italy, when that city was an independent republic and a naval power. The first denim came from Nîmes, France, hence the name denim (de Nîmes). Levi Strauss came to San Francisco in 1853 and opened up a dry-goods business. One of his many customers was a tailor named Jacob Davis, who hit upon the idea of improving the durability of work trousers by putting metal rivets at the points of strain, such as on the pocket corners and at the base of the button fly. Jacob wrote to Levi to suggest that the two men hold the patent together. Originally worn by miners, farmers and cowboys, Levi's are now worn by people in all walks of life. Since Levi Strauss's time, pure cotton fabrics have given way to cotton mixed with spandex to provide stretch.

✦   ✦   ✦

Though clearly designed and marketed by Jews, jeans are still fundamentally a non-Jewish garment. No self-respecting Jew wears stretch material which accentuates the genitalia* when comfortable cotton and wool trousers – proper schmattes – are available.

* See *Kalooki Nights* by Howard Jacobson, Cape, 2006. 'It is considered inappropriate by Jews to show strangers of either sex the outline of your glans penis.'

Having said that, some notable Jews have made money and reputations playing with this synthetic nonsense. These include:

Calvin Klein
Donna Karan
Isaac Mizrahi
Ralph Lauren
Marc Jacobs
Nicole Farhi

Schlemiel enough to pay these prices? You must be good for the Jews. Jewish tailors have always had a good living as long as they target non-Jews as their primary market. There is an old joke in the rag trade which goes like this: a Gentile goes into a clothing store and says, 'This is a very fine jacket. How much is it?' The salesman says, 'It's £500.' The Gentile says, 'OK, I'll take it.'

---

backlash + impact x j-factor = tzurus ÷ kabbalah = good/not good
3.0   + 6.25 x 7   = 64.75 ÷ 7   = 9.25

✴ **JEANS ARE GOOD FOR THE JEWS.**

JEWS FOR JESUS Moishe Rosen officially founded Jews for Jesus in September of 1973 in San Francisco, although its headquarters boast of a start date of AD 32. Today, Jews for Jesus is an international ministry with a staff of 214 spread out over eleven countries and twenty cities. Its website states, 'We believe that Jesus the Messiah was eternally pre-existent and is co-equal with God the Father; that He took on Himself the nature of man through the virgin birth.' In other words, these Jews believe that Jesus was the Messiah and that their duty is to spread this message. The group has been branded as a cult, and the website exjewsforjesus.org warns of certain suspect practices such as 'pain training' and 'shunning' in evidence.

✦ ✦ ✦

Touchy subject this.

Are Jews for Jesus trying to have it all? One day it's 'an eye for an eye', next it's 'turn the other cheek'. Makes for a messy face.

On the other hand, Jesus was Jewish so why be ashamed of it? After all, Jews have been blamed for his death by everyone from Matthew to Mel Gibson, so why not take credit for the upside of this story? And his mother was a virgin – what Jewish father could ask for more of his daughter?

If we take away the thorny issue of the crucifixion and the fact the Jews believe the Messiah hasn't come yet, Jews for Jesus has a lot in common with some Hasidic sects. Both enjoy lots of religious holidays (J4Js get double the amount!) and both believe the Messiah has come already – followers of the Lubavitcher Rebbe, Menachem Schneerson, published huge newspaper ads and rented billboards to tell everyone that their rabbi was the promised Messiah – hesitating only when he died on 12 June, 1994, at age ninety-two, and wasn't, er, actually, the Messiah. Well, not yet, anyway.

---

backlash + impact x j-factor = tzurus ÷ kabbalah = good/not good

7   + 3.1   x 3.5   = 35.35 ÷ 7   = 5.05

JEWS FOR JESUS ARE NOT GOOD FOR THE JEWS.

JEW OR FALSE?

Here's a little breather game for the amateur Judologist. Which of the following has one or more Jewish parent or grandparent?

a) Harrison Ford (actor)
b) Sean Penn (actor)
c) Ron Jeremy (porn star)
d) Harvey Keitel (actor)
e) Michael Landon (actor)
f) Ralph Lauren (designer)
g) Nostradamus (fortune-teller)
h) Nina Hartley (porn star)
i) Danielle Steele (bestselling author)
j) Vanessa Feltz (TV and radio presenter)
k) Walter Moseley (crime writer)
l) Gwyneth Paltrow (actress)

m) Jennifer Connelly (actress)

n) Adrien Brody (actor)

o) Lindsey Vuolo (porn star)

p) Maureen Lipman (actress)

Answer: All of them! They are all Jews!

JEWS WHO ARE GOOD FOR THE JEWS

Alan Greenspan (born 6 March 1926 in New York) Chairman of the Federal Reserve from 1987 to 2005, Greenspan was a very good sax player who happened to know a thing or two about interest rates. He straddled the Reagan, Bush, Clinton and Bush Jr administrations like a colossus. His word was law. During his eighteen-year span he weathered Black Monday in October 1987, saw the creation of 27 million new jobs and a rise in spending per capita of 44 per cent and experienced only two recessions. He ditched the Milton Friedman doctrine in 1996, and several countries around the world followed suit, copying his low-interest fetish. Greenspan retired in 2006, picking up a healthy $8.5 million for his memoirs from Penguin publishers. He was succeeded by Benjamin Shalom Bernanke. The markets breathed an anti-Semitic sigh of relief that another Jew wouldn't give away the family jewels.

Mark Spitz (born 10 February 1950 in Modesto, California) In his early years he didn't quite live up to the name of his hometown – he predicted he would win six gold medals in the 1968 Olympics. In fact, he won two. In the 1972 Munich games he won seven golds in the butterfly and freestyle, so best not to tease him too much. A sporting legend. Two words not used about Jews since David slew Goliath.

Judith Resnick (born 5 April 1949 in Akron, Ohio; died 28 January 1986) This granddaughter of a rabbi became the first Jewish astronaut and the second woman ever to travel in space. After her trip on the space-shuttle *Discovery* in 1984, she was picked for the fateful *Challenger* shuttle expedition which resulted in the death of all seven crew members. She is also the only Jewish person ever to have a crater on Venus named after her.

Fiorello La Guardia (born 11 December 1882 in New York; died 20 September 1947) The American politician famous for being the only Jew to have a US airport named after him. A certain pleasure must be had from the thought that some of the world's most ferociously anti-Semitic terrorists have flown into this Jewish airport. After the First World War he served several terms in Congress and opposed prohibition and supported child labour laws as well as votes for women. He served as mayor of New York from 1933, where he ended years of corruption, cleared the slums and created low-cost housing.

JEWS WHO ARE NOT GOOD FOR THE JEWS

Bugsy Siegel (Benjamin Siegelbaum) (Born 28 February 1906 in Brooklyn; died, June 1947, shot) Murder Inc.'s representative in the sunshine state. Famed for seeing the huge potential in Las Vegas as a gambling mecca; through gentle persuasion (extortion) and clever finance deals (exortion), Bugsy built the Flamingo Hotel, which would be the centre of world gambling. Unfortunately, he skimmed too much off the top (you just can't get good accountants in Nevada) and was bumped off. Pioneer or playboy?

Bruno Kreisky (born 22 January 1911 in Vienna; died 1990) The chancellor of Austria 1970–83. Yes, you heard right, Austria. A Jew as chancellor of the most anti-Semitic country in Europe must be taken seriously. Not wishing to be seen as too Jewish, he appointed four former Nazis to his cabinet, was very happy to include war criminals in his coalition (Friedrich Peter, the far-right leader who was exposed as a member of a troupe that murdered thousands of Jews), and was one of the first European leaders to welcome Yasser Arafat. Self-hating or visionary statesman?

Meyer 'The Brain' Lansky (Majer Suchowlinski) (born 4 July 1902 in Grodno, Poland; died 15 January 1983 of lung cancer) This murdering gangster holds a special place in the hearts of Judologists everywhere as his lifelong motto was 'Is it good for Meyer?'

He went into business with Lucky Luciano, and they formed the National Crime Syndicate, though it was unusual for non-Italians to be allowed entry. Lansky operated in Cuba, Florida and Vegas on gambling projects and the character Hyman Roth in *The Godfather II* is based on him. Despite fleeing to Israel and 'donating' millions to the Zionist cause, he was sent packing in 1972, but was acquitted in a US court in 1973 of a charge of tax evasion. One positive result of his sojourn in the Promised Land was a tightening-up of the Law of Return. He was said to have amassed $100 million from drugs, gambling and prostitution. Enterprising businessman with multi-cultural links or murdering shyster?

JEWS* WHO WOULD BE GOOD TO MARRY

(Eligibility ratings are out of seven – naturally – with seven being optimum desirability and one being its opposite.)

The girls

Scarlett Johansson (born 22 November 1984 in New York) American star of *Girl with a Pearl Earring*, *Lost in Translation* and *Match Point*. Don't be misled by her Danish father: look to her mother, Melanie Sloan, for the J-factor. As if things could not get better, she faced

* Defined as having one or more Jewish parents/grandparents. The subject may not even know he or she is Jewish.

off Tom Cruise on Scientology and was dropped from *Mission Impossible III* as a result.

Judological eligibility rating: 7

Neve Adrianne Campbell (born 3 October 1973 in Ontario). She moved from teen actress in the TV show *Party of Five* to a leading role in the film *Scream*. Known for her no-nudity clauses, so possibly good for frum Jews? However, she does identify herself now as a Catholic, so might not be ideal for baale teshuvim.

Judological eligibility rating: 4.5

Sophie Okonedo (born 1 Janury 1969 in London). Oscar-nominated star of *Hotel Rwanda*. When asked why she shunned all the glamorous Hollywood parties she'd been invited to, she replied that she couldn't get a good babysitter. Heimische.

Judological eligibility rating: 3.5

Winona Ryder (born Winona Laura Horowitz, 29 October 1971 in Winona, Minnesota). As famous for her roles in *Aliens*, *Heathers* and *The Crucible* as she is for shop-lifting and having numerous boyfriends. Trouble with a capital T.

Judological eligibility rating: 2.5

Monica Samille Lewinsky (born 23 July 1973 in San Francisco). Her fame revolves around a blue dress with semen stains and a cigar that went into the wrong orifice. Nothing wrong with that.

Judological eligibility rating: 7

The boys

David Blaine (born David Blaine White, 4 April 1973 in Brooklyn, New York). He would be a strange date as he is used to locking himself in ice, starving himself above the Thames and standing on very tall pillars for extraordinary lengths of time. Still, he is clearly the kind of guy who sticks around.

Judological eligibility rating: 4

Harvey Weinstein (born 19 March 1952 in Queens). If you are in search of a big personality in a big frame, look no further. Not for the sensitive, as he is known for his huge temper, undiminished by his crash dieting, and his, shall we say, 'focus'. Hugely successful and must be applauded for naming his company Miramax after his mom and pa, Miriam and Max. Nice Jewish boy.

Judological eligibility rating: 4

Sergey Mihailovich Brin (born August 1973 in Moscow). Co-founder of Google, has an estimated wealth of $11 billion, which makes him very eligible. But before any Jewish female readers feel the need to call him up for a date, be warned that small talk with Sergey might well involve phrases like 'gagillions' and 'entangled nuclear spins'.

Judological eligibility rating: 5.5

Boris Becker (born 22 November 1967 in Leiman, Germany). One of the great tennis players, he has a penchant for the ladies. Born on the same day (different year) as Scarlett Johansson, so that sorts his pick-up line. One tip: if he asks you to go into the broom cupboard at the restaurant on your first date, don't go. Last time he did this at Nobu, in London, his five-minute exchange of fluids resulted in a little Becker and a huge child-maintenance bill. On second thoughts, if you date Boris, go straight to the broom cupboard.

Judological eligibility rating: 6

Joaquin Rafael Phoenix (born 28 October 1974 in Puerto Rico). Also known as Leaf, so clearly suitable for the outdoor type of girl. Famous for his roles in *Gladiator* and *Walk the Line*. Although he has a Jewish-born mother, his parents weren't exactly Shomer Shabbos as they belonged to the Children of God. So, if you are relaxed about which family to go to on Rosh Hashanah, this guy is for you.

Judological eligibility rating: 3.5

KARMA (Sanskrit, from the root *kri*, 'to do') A concept central to Eastern religion (Hinduism, Sikhism, Buddhism and Jainism). It means that the actions a person takes or the thoughts a person has throughout their life directly affect what happens to him or her in this life and in subsequent lives. It refers to the cycle of cause and effect. A person who commits good acts has good karma, a person who commits bad acts has bad karma. Karma may not come to fruition in a person's lifetime but may occur in rebirth, so a good person may be reincarnated to a superior life and a bad person may be reincarnated to an inferior life, e.g. as an animal.

✦ ✦ ✦

Deuteronomy 19:21 says, 'Life shall go for life, eye for eye, tooth for tooth' – not exactly what the ancient Easterns meant by karma, but a Jewish version nonetheless.

Jews have been drawn to Buddhism since the sixties, and in the San Francisco Bay area there are many Jewish Buddhist teachers who see a compatibility between notions of suffering and spiritual solace. They also smoke a lot of dope in the Bay area, so they have plenty of time to sit around saying things like 'shit happens'.

Jews who have seen the Eastern light are now called JUBUs, and there are many famous JUBUs: Leonard Cohen, Goldie Hawn, Steven Seagal, Allen Ginsberg and David Ben Gurion. An old JUBU story tells of how a Jewish mother spent six months trekking up a Nepalese mountain to seek an audience with the holy guru, Master Shin-Yeng Lu, only to say three words when she finally reached the summit: 'Herschel, come home.'

Jews and karma have a rocky relationship. After all, who is going to argue that the 5,000 years of suffering was brought about by things they did when they were small? Mind you, it is quite a challenge to think how gangsters like Bugsy Siegel or Meyer Lansky will be reincarnated. What is in store for villains like Robert Maxwell, Leopold and Loeb, Jack Abramoff and Arnold Rothstein? What animal will be honoured by bearing Yigal Amir's soul? It is not just villains who are susceptible to reincarnation. Consider Joan Rivers, the comedienne who has returned as a mad cow.

---

backlash + impact x j-factor = tzurus ÷ kabbalah = good/not good
5.9   + 4.5   x 5.1   = 53.04 ÷ 7   = 7.58

✹ KARMA IS BORDERLINE AND THERE-FORE NOT GOOD FOR THE JEWS.

KY JELLY A water-based personal lubricant produced by Johnson & Johnson. It was created in 1917 and was known then as Jelly Personal Lubricant. No one knows why it is called KY Jelly. Some believe it is because it was created in Kentucky (hence KY). It was not available over the counter until 1980. It was first marketed only to doctors for use during pelvic examinations of female patients and today is mainly used as a sexual lubricant. It contains no colours or perfumes and is water-soluble. (Source: K-Y website.)

◆　◆　◆

The age-old debate as to whether sexual intercourse is better with or without a circumcised penis rages on. There is a strong case to be argued that the friction caused by a circumcised member during intercourse removes the natural lubricants of the female of the species and therefore KY Jelly is a necessary aid to fulfilling the mitzvah of pleasuring one's wife.

Lubrication, at first glance, might not seem a particularly edifying topic of discussion for the serious Judologist, but sex is widely discussed in the Torah. In fact, Genesis makes it clear that sex is linked to knowledge – the Hebrew word *yada* means *knowing* and Adam *knew* Eve (a holy nudge nudge, wink wink) and they ate from the Tree of Knowledge (geddit?). Sex is serious business. So what's wrong with getting it right?

Willhelm Reich argued in his book *The Function of the Orgasm* (1927) that failure to reach orgasm can lead to neurosis. Another argument for KY in every Jewish household? However, before logging on to annsummers.com, remember: Judaism is about fertility rather than eroticism. Medieval Ashkenazis sought an erotic link to the Primary Mover rather than focusing their attention on the baser, corporeal experience. Puts the phrase 'did the earth move for you?' into historical perspective. It can also explain many young Jewish males' belief that they are God's gift to women.

Warning: applying KY Jelly is a very messy procedure which can be off-putting for Jewish women who can't bear untidy bedrooms and are used to getting a handyman to do everything for them.

---

backlash + impact x j-factor = tzurus ÷ kabbalah = good/not good

2   + 4.45 x 2.4   = 15.48 ÷ 7   = 2.21

✹ **KY JELLY IS NOT GOOD FOR THE JEWS.**

L

LAWSON, NIGELLA (Born 6 January 1960) A cookery writer, journalist and television presenter. She is the daughter of the former chancellor of the exchequer Nigel Lawson and the late society beauty Vanessa Salmon. Her brother, Dominic Lawson, was formerly the editor of the *Sunday Telegraph*. She is the author of five bestsellers, *How to Eat* (1999), *Nigella Bites* (2001), *How to Be a Domestic Goddess* (2003), *Feast* (2004) and *Forever Summer* (2005).

◆ ◆ ◆

Anyone who describes a simple raspberry as 'slut-red' is welcome in my house.

Nigella, with her feminized father's name, is perhaps the ultimate Jewish fantasy figure. To women, she is an intelligent, sensual woman who enjoys her curves. To men she is an intelligent, sensual women whose curves you want to enjoy.

Nigella's Jewishness is not necessarily central to her cooking. However, she does like to mix and match ethnic dishes. It is not uncommon to see her licking her lips erotically while pummelling gefilte fish into shape. The question on Judologists' minds must be: what effect does this siren of the stove have on the

Jewish psyche? Is she the ultimate balebooste figure with the tzimmis always simmering at the ready? Or is she the Lilith of the latkes ready to pour bread sauce over your vermicelli? Is she Golda from *Fiddler on the Roof* or Sharon Stone from *Basic Instinct*?

Well, she does cook Jewish dishes, but has been known to recommend them after serious treyf. For example, her wonderful lokshen pudding, the recipe for which appears in *Feast*, is recommended to follow roast loin pork. Like Moses, she leads you to the Promised Land, but won't take you there. She has also been known to say, 'Christmas isn't complete if you haven't got a ham as well as a turkey.' Boy, does she know how to drive a young Jewish boy mad.

---

backlash + impact x j-factor = tzurus ÷ kabbalah = good/not good

4.25   + 5.75   x 6.9   = 69   ÷ 7   = 9.85

☀ **NIGELLA IS GOOD FOR THE JEWS.**

LAWYER A professional person authorized to practise law who conducts lawsuits or gives legal advice. Western law can be said to have its origins in the Old Testament, when, in approximately 1300 BC, Moses received a list of ten laws directly from God. The first recorded legal ruling came in 1850 BC, when Hammurabi, King of Babylon, developed the oldest existing code of laws.

◆ ◆ ◆

There are countless jokes made at the expense of lawyers painting them as liars, cheats and extortionists. How can you tell when a lawyer is lying? His lips are moving. You're trapped in a room with a tiger, a rattlesnake and a lawyer. Your gun has only two bullets. What should you do? Shoot the lawyer – *twice*. And so on. Why, then, is the law so attractive to Jewish mothers as a career path for their offspring? Is it good for the Jews that Jews are prominent in such a maligned profession?

At heart, Judaism is an argument over the law, so why not make a living out of it? In the Bible there are 613 mitzvot (commandments) and books and books of commentary on these laws in the Mishnah and Gemara, so Jews are trained from an early age to hone their analytical skills. But do they have to keep you on the phone so long?

Lawyers are not all venal. Many Jews have been important figures in the civil rights movement. For every two-bit shyster there is a lawyer like William Kunstler, who fought for Lenny Bruce, Malcolm X, the Native Americans and many more. It must be noted that the desire for litigation can rebound on even the most noble of lawsuits. For example, lawyers helped in the suit against the Swiss government to reclaim some of the stolen gold of Holocaust survivors. Not to be outdone, there is now a lawsuit from Egyptian lawyers planning to sue 'all the Jews of the world' over gold that was allegedly stolen during the biblical exodus of the Israelites from Egypt. Dr Nabil

Hilmi, Dean of the Faculty of Law at the University of Al-Zaqaziq, argues that the Israelites stole jewelry and cooking utensils, fleeing in the middle of the night with all this wealth and not even leaving a thank-you note.

---

backlash + impact x j-factor = tzurus ÷ kabbalah = good/not good
6.57   + 3.45 x 5.25 = 52.6 ÷ 7   = 7.51

LAWYERS ARE BORDERLINE AND THEREFORE NOT GOOD FOR THE JEWS.

LEWINSKY, MONICA In 1995 Monica Lewinsky was an intern at the White House. In January of 1998 a tape was released of a conversation between Monica and Pentagon employee Linda Tripp which revealed Lewinsky and President Bill Clinton were conducting an illicit affair. The president was impeached when he was forced to admit the 'inappropriate relationship'. Lewinsky later started a new career as a handbag designer and is currently studying at the London School of Economics.

•　•　•

'I did not have sexual relations with that woman,' were the words spoken by President Clinton to the media at the height of the scandal. Faint echoes of 'There will be no whitewash in the White House' made twenty years earlier by President Nixon? Both statements turned out to be sophistry, as 'no sex' meant 'a blow-job and playing around with a cigar' and 'no whitewash' meant 'complete and utter whitewash'.

Is Monica a dream intern/employee or a Jewish princess nightmare? The jury is out because some might argue that President Clinton was interested not so much in her Jewish identity as her Jewish mouth. As the following quotes from a Syrian newspaper show, her Jewishness did seem relevant to some people:

Monica is a Jewess, the lawyers who volunteered to defend her were Jews, Monica's friends who recorded the hot phone conversations between her and President Clinton were Jewesses and the *Washington Post* newspaper which published the affair for the first time is a Jewish newspaper . . .
(*Tishrin Al-Usbu'a, 24 August 1998*)

Monica will sadly go down in history as the one with the cigar, and for this reason her legacy to world Jewry is not wholly positive. Having said that, many Jews are still amazed to hear of a Jewish woman on her knees, even once.

She is also responsible for renaming the Jew's harp (a small lyre-shaped instrument that is placed between the teeth and played by twanging a wire tongue while changing the shape of the mouth cavity) to Monica's harp, which is good for the Jews.

---

backlash + impact x j-factor = tzurus ÷ kabbalah = good/not good

5.5   + 5.45   x 7   = 76.65 ÷ 7   = 10.95

 MONICA LEWINSKY IS GOOD FOR THE JEWS.

LITERATURE: WRITERS WHO ARE NOT GOOD FOR THE JEWS

If you are the type of person who can no longer enjoy great works of literature if you learn negative things about your favourite authors, then please skip this section. All the below were not good for the Jews. Their Judological rating is given beneath each entry. Remember, the lower the number, the less good this writer is for the Jews.

Roald Dahl (1916–90) Author of *James and the Giant Peach* (1961), *The Twits* (1980), *The BFG* (1982) and *Matilda* (1988). Dahl once told a journalist, 'There's a trait in the Jewish character that does provoke animosity . . . I mean there is always a reason why anti-anything crops up anywhere; even a stinker like Hitler didn't just pick on them for no reason.' This slip of the tongue – for what else could it be? – lost him his chance of a knighthood and made him even more embittered against the Jews. After all, the Child-catcher in *Chitty Chitty Bang Bang*, the movie he scripted, was nothing like a stereotype of a Jew – black hat, long black coat and huge pointy nose. Some Judologists have argued that his most popular book, *Charlie and the Chocolate Factory*, can be read as a very dark fable – innocent children tricked into a concentration camp complex manned by strange sub-humans who take them away one by one – but the Institute would like to distance itself from such a position.

Judological rating: 2.25

Mark Twain (1835–1910) Author of *The Adventures of Huckleberry Finn* (1885) and *The Adventures of Tom Sawyer* (1876). Twain wrote of Jews as 'simple, superstitious, disease-tortured creatures' who could only understand a transcendental idea 'if it was written on their skins'.

Judological rating: 2.75

Ernest Hemingway (1899–1961) Author of *The Sun Also Rises* (1926), *To Have and Have Not* (1937) and *For Whom the Bell Tolls* (1940). Hemingway often ranted about 'kikes' in his letters. This often translated into less-than-flattering 'Jew' characters such as Robert Cohn in *The Sun Also Rises* and self-indulgent tirades against Jews in stories such as 'Fifty Grand'.

Judological rating: 3.25

Charles Dickens (1812–70) Author of *The Adventures of Oliver Twist* (1838), *David Copperfield* (1850) and *Bleak House* (1853). In the first thirty-eight chapters of *Oliver Twist* there are 257 references to 'the Jew' against forty-two to 'Fagin'. Dickens described Fagin as 'villainous looking and repulsive' and made no secret that he was based on Jews of that period when he claimed 'that class of criminal almost invariably was a Jew'. However, he did redeem himself with *Our Mutual Friend*, where he presented the noble character of Riah, an elderly Jew who looks after downcast young women. In a letter Dickens said, 'There is nothing but good will left between me and a People for whom I have a real regard.' Some of my best friends are . . .

Judological rating: 3.75

Kingsley Amis (1922–95) Author of *Lucky Jim* (1954), *Girl, 20* (1971) and *The Old Devils* (1986). He was once asked by an interviewer whether he was anti-Semitic. 'Very, very mildly,' replied Amis. Pressed to elaborate, he offered this: 'Well, when I'm watching the credits roll at the end of a TV programme, I say to myself: "Oh, there's another one."'

Judological rating: 4.2

Agatha Christie (1890–1976) Author of *Murder at the Vicarage* (1930), *Murder on the Orient Express* (1934) and *Death on the Nile* (1937). In *The Mysterious*

Mr Quinn, this lovely description of Jews is included: 'men of Hebraic extraction, sallow men with hooked noses, wearing flamboyant jewellery'.

Peril at End House has a character referred to as 'the long-nosed Mr Lazarus', of whom somebody says, 'he's a Jew, of course, but a frightfully decent one'. The original title of *And Then There Were None* was, of course, *Ten Little Niggers*, which might reflect an underlying attitude to people of other races.

Judological rating: 3.95

Dorothy L. Sayers (1893–1957) Creator of Lord Peter Wimsey. In the 1940s, she wrote an essay in *The Future of the Jews* by J. J. Lynx, in which she argued that Jews are bad citizens with little or no loyalty to the country they live in.

Judological rating: 4.3

Graham Greene (1904–91) Author of *Brighton Rock* (1938), *The Third Man* (1950) and *The End of the Affair* (1951). 'She deserved something better than a man named Furtstein . . . The domed Semitic forehead, the dark eyes over the rather gaudy tie' (*The Confidential Agent*). 'How the financial crisis has improved English films! They have lost their tasteless Semitic opulence and are becoming – English' (*The Spectator*, 7 April 1939).

Judological rating: 5.0

F. Scott Fitzgerald (1896–1940) Author of *The Beautiful and the Damned* (1922), *The Great Gatsby* (1925) and *Tender Is the Night* (1934). In *The Great Gatsby* the narrator encounters Gatsby's friend, Meyer Wolfsheim, a dodgy gambler who 'fixed the World Series in 1919'. The narrator describes him as 'a small, flat-nosed Jew' who 'raised his large head and regarded me with two fine growths of hair which luxuriated in either nostril. After a moment I discovered his tiny eyes in the half-darkness.' Every description of Wolfsheim that follows refers to his nose: he 'covered Gatsby with his expressive nose', 'Mr Wolfsheim's nose flashed at me indignantly', 'His nostrils turned to me in an interesting way', 'As he turned away his tragic nose was trembling'.

Judological rating: 3.75

John Fowles (1926–2005) Author of *The Collector* (1963), *The Magus* (1965) and *The French Lieutenant's Woman* (1969).

In his diaries, Fowles said of his publisher Tom Maschler that 'of all the Jews I know he is the most Jewish: the perfect example of the bitter, wandering, cast-out son of Israel'. Milton Shulman, the theatre critic, was also described in such terms as a man who has 'that Canadian Jewish love of being outrageous, a little comical, as talk-monopolising as Dr Johnson . . . These people (this state of mind) have far too much power.' Shame, I liked *The Magus*.

Judological rating: 4.65

LIVINGSTONE, KENNETH ROBERT (Born 17 June 1945, Lambeth) Ken Livingstone held council positions for Labour in Lambeth and Camden from 1971 to 1981. He became leader of the GLC (Greater London Council) from 1981 until its abolition by Margaret Thatcher in 1986. Never shy of controversy, he was one of the first elected officials to invite a representative of Sinn Fein to the GLC and campaigned for gay rights. Labelled 'Red Ken' for his left-wing views, he was described by the *Sun* newspaper as 'the most odious man in Britain'. Since 4 May 2000, he has been London's Mayor, having been re-elected in 2004.

◆　◆　◆

EXT. Night. Outside a party for ex-minister Chris Smith.

Oliver Finegold, journalist, approaches Ken Livingstone, the Mayor of London.

FINEGOLD: Mr Livingstone, *Evening Standard.* How did tonight go?

LIVINGSTONE: How awful for you. Have you thought of having treatment?

FINEGOLD: How did tonight go?

LIVINGSTONE: Have you thought of having treatment?

FINEGOLD: Was it a good party? What does it mean for you?

LIVINGSTONE: What did you do before? Were you a German war criminal?

FINEGOLD: No, I'm Jewish, I wasn't a German war criminal and I'm actually quite offended by that. So, how did tonight go?

LIVINGSTONE: Arr right, well you might be [Jewish], but actually you are just like a concentration camp guard, you are just doing it because you are paid to, aren't you?

FINEGOLD: Great, I have you on record for that. So, how was tonight?

LIVINGSTONE: It's nothing to do with you because your paper is a load of scumbags and reactionary bigots.

FINEGOLD: I'm a journalist and I'm doing my job. I'm only asking for a comment.

LIVINGSTONE: Well, work for a paper that doesn't have a record of supporting Fascism.

Mayor Livingstone then walks off.

(Transcript in *Evening Standard*, 8 February 2005)

Sorry yet, Ken?

---

backlash + impact x j-factor = tzurus ÷ kabbalah = good/not good

1.5   + 1.5   x 0.1   = 0.3 ÷ 7   = 0.04

✺ **MAYOR LIVINGSTONE IS NOT GOOD FOR THE JEWS.**

LLOYD WEBBER, ANDREW (Born 22 March 1948) Lloyd Webber is arguably the most popular and successful British composer of musical theatre of the late twentieth century, with multiple musicals that have run for more than a decade both on Broadway and in the West End. In 2005, Lloyd Webber sold four of the twelve West End theatres that he had 50 per cent stakes in to Broadway producer Max Weitzenhoffer and Nica Burns.

◆ ◆ ◆

Joseph and the Amazing Technicolor Dreamcoat was the first musical theatre show written by the team of Andrew Lloyd Webber and Tim Rice. This musical retelling of the Joseph story is undoubtedly positive for the Jews and includes the following advice to Joseph from Pharaoh:

> *Find a man to lead you through the famine*
> *With a flair for economic planning*

which inspired a generation of accountants.

It is not this sympathetic rags-to-riches rendering of how the first Jew became CFO of Egypt, but Lloyd Webber's second work, *Jesus Christ Superstar*, that presents possible areas of concern for the Judologist. Clearly, any depiction of Judas Iscariot in mainstream culture is not great for the Jews. And do they have to go on about it? Eight performances a week, all over the world. It was 2,000 years ago.

The final nail in the coffin for the richest composer

in the world must be one of his biggest successes, 1981's *Cats*. The lyrics were based on T. S. Eliot's 1939 *Old Possum's Book of Practical Cats*, which Lloyd Webber confessed was a childhood favourite. Before 9 January 2006, when *Phantom of the Opera* took over the mantle, *Cats* had been the longest-running Broadway musical, spanning a reign of more than twenty years. T. S. Eliot was a notorious anti-Semite who famously said in a lecture at the University of Virginia in 1933, 'Reasons of race and religion combine to make any large number of free-thinking Jews undesirable.' There is also the famous line in his poem of 1920 'Burbank with a Baedeker: Bleistein with a Cigar' which compares Jews to rats. Mmmm.

---

backlash + impact x j-factor = tzurus ÷ kabbalah = good/not good
4   + 4   x 1   = 8   ÷ 7   = 1.14

✳ **ANDREW LLOYD WEBBER'S MUSICALS ARE NOT GOOD FOR THE JEWS.**

MADONNA Madonna (born Louise Ciccone in Bay City, Michigan, 16 August 1958) is an American singer frequently referred to as the queen of pop music. Many consider Madonna to be one of the most iconic figures of the late twentieth century.

* * *

Madonna is the most famous member of the Kabbalah Centre. Madonna adopted a Hebrew name – Esther – but she was born a Catholic, and many Orthodox Jews believe a non-Jew has no place studying Kabbalah. Strictly speaking, it is forbidden for non-Jews, women and all men under the age of forty to learn Kabbalah. Kabbalah is regarded by some as the highest form of Judaism, and those who practise it need to be extremely spiritual, modest and wise, surrounding themselves with holiness and purity. Her hit song 'Like a Virgin' (1984) is a strong positive signal in this direction, but unfortunately 'Hanky Panky' (in the film *Dick Tracy*, 1990) might well have damaged her case somewhat.

Kabbalah, which means 'that which is received', is a name for the arcane works of Jewish mysticism that were first set down in the Middle Ages and collected in thirteenth century Spain. Its theoretical content is regarded as profound, if esoteric, but its practical applications border on the magical. Even very observant Jews seldom dip in.

The word Madonna has seven letters. As we've seen, the number seven has special spiritual significance in Judology. There are seven days of the week; Yom Kippur and Rosh Hashanah occur in the seventh month of the Hebrew calendar; there are seven Laws of Noah; the Torah begins with a verse containing seven words; when a close relative dies, we sit shiva for seven days; Moses was the seventh generation after Abraham; God created seven levels of heaven (hence the expression, 'I'm in seventh heaven!'); the world has seven continents. Think about it: coincidence?

The other argument is that she kissed a black Jesus surrounded by burning crosses. That is chutzpah.

---

backlash + impact x j-factor = tzurus ÷ kabbalah = good/not good
5.56   + 3.15 x 2.89 = 25.17 ÷ 7   = 3.59

☀ **MADONNA IS NOT GOOD FOR THE JEWS.**

MARIJUANA OR CANNABIS A drug produced from the dried leaves and flowers of the hemp plant. It is thought to have medicinal as well as psychoactive effects, and there is evidence that it has been in use since ancient times. Effects vary and include: increased appetite, dry mouth, euphoria, paranoia and short-term memory loss. Also called pot, spliff or ganja. It was criminalized across most of the world in the early twentieth century and continues to be so to this day. (Source: wikipedia.org.)

*   *   *

Pot can increase paranoia, which, frankly, is all the Jews need.

There is a hippy side to the Kabbalah which appeals to pot-smoking frumers who wish to connect with the divine energy flow and many a Hanukkah table has chamantashen hash cakes for the over-barmitzvahs.

Theories abound that Jesus used cannabis ointment to help with his healing abilities. The recipe for anointing oil, recorded in Exodus (30:23–5), includes *kaneh-bosm*, phonetically similar to 'cannabis', and most in the archaeology community agree that hashish has been around for 1,600 years. A reference to *qeneh* in Isaiah 43:24 refers to a 'sweet-tasting' plant. I'm really not sure what kind of shit he was taking there, but Isaiah was a trippy guy.

The Bible makes countless references to people getting stoned.

President Nixon should have the final word. 'You know,' he said to Bob Haldeman, 'it's a funny thing, every one of the bastards that are out for legalizing marijuana is Jewish. What the Christ is the matter with the Jews, Bob? What is the matter with them? I suppose it is because most of them are psychiatrists.' (Source: *Washington Post*.)

---

backlash + impact x j-factor = tzurus ÷ kabbalah = good/not good
5.23   + 6.01   x 6.0   = 67.44 ÷ 7   = 9.63

 ## MARIJUANA/CANNABIS IS GOOD FOR THE JEWS.

MOUSTACHE, THE A growth of facial hair on the upper lip most often worn by men, though occasionally they also adorn women. Moustaches come in different shapes and sizes, for example the pencil moustache (Errol Flynn, John Waters), the Dali (as in Salvador), natural, walrus, handlebar, Wild West, Fu Manchu or imperial.

◆ ◆ ◆

Can the type of moustache you wear be good for the Jews? The small box-shaped 'tache was made famous by Adolf Hitler (1889–1945) yet ridiculed in the same era by Charlie Chaplin (1889–1977). The pleasure one derives from defacing a famous politician's visage on a poster by drawing a 'Hitler moustache' must also not be underestimated.

Another famous moustache-wearer was Joseph Stalin (1879–1953), the Soviet dictator, whose moustache was large and walrus-like but well kempt, rather like that of a modern-day tyrant, Saddam Hussein (1937–). The moustache choice of these brutal megalomaniacs cannot be seen as proof of anti-Semitism:

the walrus look was also used by Albert Einstein (1879–1955). Although he turned down the job of President of the state of Israel, Professor Einstein's moustache was not part of the decision. At least he bothered to grow his own walrus, which is more than can be said of Groucho Marx (1890–1977), who sprayed his on. He did go on to grow one for real in his dotage, but the damage had been done.

Does a beard diminish the power of the moustache? When Saddam Hussein was discovered in a hole after losing the second Gulf War, what shocked the world was not so much his thin, gaunt expression as his unbearable hirsuteness. In fact, he looked like a Sephardic rabbi after Yom Kippur. He continued to sport the beard/moustache combo in captivity and perhaps sealed his fate?

There are countless other world leaders who have affected Jewish life who have unashamedly sported moustaches. Lech Walesa, Marshal Pétain, Golda Meir, to name but a few. Neville Chamberlain (1869–1940), the British Prime Minister who limited immigration of Jews to Palestine in the 1930s and did a deal with Hitler in 1938, provides a good example of a natural-looking moustache that had dire effects on world Jewry. Perhaps the most famous facial hair in history was that of Esau in the Bible, who was the victim of a double theft by his twin brother – his birthright and father's blessing – and then as victim of this hostile takeover was forced to accept the accession of Jacob as Father of the Jewish Nation. Hair does not seem to get you far. Also, he was a ginger.

backlash + impact x j-factor = tzurus ÷ kabbalah = good/not good
4   + 5   x 4   = 36   ÷ 7   = 5.14

THE MOUSTACHE IS NOT GOOD FOR THE JEWS.

MOVIES THAT ARE GOOD FOR THE JEWS

Tora! Tora! Tora! (1970, dir. Richard Fleischer and Kinji Fukasaku, starring Martin Balsam and Sô Yamamura). One letter away from being a decent movie.

The Taking of Pelham One, Two, Three (1974, dir. Joseph Sargent, starring Walther Matthau, Robert Shaw and Martin Balsam again). The only mainstream movie in the seventies to have a Jewish detective who ends with a Yiddish word ('gesundheit'). Martin Balsam is Jewish too.

Marathon Man (1976, dir. John Schlesinger, starring Dustin Hoffman and Laurence Olivier). Jew as good athlete. Inspiring. Also, for once, the truth about dentists.

The Passion of the Christ (2004, dir. Mel Gibson, starring James Caviezel, Maia Morgenstern and Monica Bellucci). Well, it can't get worse for Jews after a film like this. Besides, Mel Gibson told *Fox News* that his next project was going to be the story of the Maccabees, so it can't be all bad.

Pulp Fiction (1994, dir. Quentin Tarantino, starring John Travolta, Samuel L. Jackson). Ezekiel is quoted liberally throughout the film and Jackson's character does not eat pork.

Life of Brian (1979, dir. Terry Jones, starring the Monty Python team). At last, the truth. Should be seen in a double bill with *The Passion of the Christ*, if possible.

The Big Lebowski (1998, dir. Joel Coen, starring Jeff Bridges, John Goodman). Where else can you find a non-Jewish psychopath who is 'Shomer Shabbos'?

Babe (1995, dir. Chris Noonan, starring a pig). Sales in bacon and ham dropped radically after this film was screened around the world.

Raid on Entebbe (1977, dir. Irvin Kershner, starring Charles Bronson, Peter Finch – and Martin Balsam). Ah, a time when wearing the IDF uniform and being called Yonni meant you were a hero. Martin Balsam again.

Meet the Parents (2000, dir. Jay Roach, starring Ben Stiller, Robert De Niro). A Jew causes chaos in a WASP household but still keeps the girl. Unheard of. Unthinkable.

MOVIES THAT ARE NOT GOOD FOR THE JEWS

A Stranger Among us (1992 dir. Sidney Lumet, starring Melanie Griffith). Words are insufficient to describe this cak.

Jakob the Liar (1999 dir. Peter Kassovitz, starring Robin Williams). It takes some kind of movie to make you want to keep a Jew in the Warsaw Ghetto . . .

Titanic (1997, dir. James Cameron, starring Leonardo Di Caprio, Kate Winslet). No Jews involved here, just a very very bad movie.

Once Upon a Time in America (1984, dir. Sergio Leone, starring Robert De Niro, James Woods). Jewish gangsters? Shame on all those involved. James Woods Jewish? Preposterous.

Birth of a Nation (1915, dir. D. W. Griffith, starring Lillian Gish, Ralph Lewis). About the American Civil War and the birth of the Ku Klux Klan. Very popular with Klansmen reunion charity galas.

Se7en (1995, dir. David Fincher, starring Morgan Freeman, Brad Pitt). Not a good movie for Judologists as it casts our sacred number in a poor light.

Keeping the Faith (2000, dir. Edward Norton, starring

Ben Stiller, Edward Norton). I lost mine watching this dreck.

Love Story (1970, dir. Arthur Hiller, starring Ryan O'Neal, Ali McGraw). Introduction into the mainstream of the phenomenon that is a Jewish-American princess. And he still falls for her . . .

The Chosen (1981, dir. Jeremy Kagan, starring Robert Benson, Rod Steiger). Shhh . . . don't tell everyone.

MUSICAL, THE A play or film the action and dialogue of which is interspersed with singing and dancing and where music plays an extended, primary role. *The Beggar's Opera* of 1728 is said to be the first example of musical theatre or operetta as opposed to opera. The growth in the musical occurred in the first half of the twentieth century with landmark shows such as *Annie Get Your Gun*, *Showboat*, *Carousel* and *Oklahoma*. Since the sixties, the musical has generated billions of pounds in productions such as *The Sound of Music*, *Fiddler on the Roof* and *Phantom of the Opera*.

* * *

It is not controversial to say that Jews dominated the writing, composing and production of the broadway musical in the first half of the twentieth century. One can see that many Jews, like Oscar Hammerstein, Jerome Kern, Richard Rogers, George and Ira Gershwin, Leonard Bernstein and Stephen Sondheim, influenced how Americans saw their country by using a Jewish perspective on non-Jewish subjects (ever met a Jew in Oklahoma?).

Hardly surprising, then, to discover that the composer of the biggest-selling song ever, 'White Christmas', and the huge hit movie *Easter Parade* was of course a Jew called Irving Berlin (né Israel Isidore Baline). Perhaps Izzy did not think he would make money on ditties like 'Chappy Chanukah' and 'Pesach Parade'. Mind you, Berlin's early success came with the touching song 'Yiddle on Your Fiddle' (1909), but he knew it had limited appeal. The crowning glory, though, must be his composition 'God Bless America'. Let's face it, who else could have written it? A non-Jew? Feh!

Why are Jews good at musical theatre? Perhaps with a history which is nothing to sing about, Jews turn to fantasy and song. Moments of profundity can occur in the American musical, like when Tevye, the milkman in *Fiddler on the Roof*, says, 'We are your chosen people. But, once in a while, can't you choose someone else?'

However, musical theatre tends to be about very non-Jewish subjects. Judge for yourself with this random sample of Jewish compositions:

Showboat – love on a Mississippi cruiser featuring a gambler called Gaylord.

Oklahoma – the conflict between cowboys and farmhands.

On the Town – three sailors in New York looking for a good time with no money. Looking for girls. Enough said.

West Side Story – Italians and Hispanics battle it out in a Romeo and Juliet storyline.

Brigadoon – invisible Scottish village inhabited by mad people with dodgy accents singing to Gene Kelly.

The King and I – Thai King hires opinionated, fussy woman to look after his family – actually, quite Jewish when you think about it.

The show that broke the mould and made the Broadway musical relevant, vibrant and intellectually rigorous was, of course, *The Producers*, or *Springtime for Hitler: A Gay Romp with Adolf and Eva in Berchtesgaden*, as it is known in the play and film. Mel Brooks, the show's creator, often thanked Hitler for his inspiration. In reality, his true inspiration was *A Night at the Opera*, the Marx brothers film, the central premise of which was making money out of a flop, but, as Michael Caine said when reviewing his acting career, 'if you are going to steal, steal from the best'. Many have been offended by this musical, but comedy is a typical Jewish way of dealing with tragedy, and Mel Brooks argues that jokes at Hitler's expense (à la Chaplin in *The Great Dictator*) are a way of 'laughing the Nazis into oblivion'.

---

backlash + impact x j-factor = tzurus ÷ kabbalah = good/not good
4.25   + 6.35 x 6.1   = 64.7 ÷ 7   = 9.24

 THE MUSICAL IS GOOD FOR THE JEWS.

WORLD TIMELINE
(PART III – 1095 TO 1750)

WORLD

1095–1099	1100–1200	1215	1337–1453	1350–1450	1470	1492	1498	1491–1597	1685–1750
First Crusade	Universities begin	King John signs the Magna Carta	Hundred Years War	Political chaos in Germany	William Caxton publishes first book	Columbus sails the ocean blue	Leonardo da Vinci paints *The Last Supper*	King Henry VIII has six wives	J. S. Bach and boom in classical music

JEWISH

1095–1099	1100–1200	1215	1337–1453	1350–1450	1470	1492	1498	1491–1597	1685–1750
Here We Go!	Jews begin quest for -ologies	First estate agent opens for business	Sorry, in my book that's 116 years	Now, there's a surprise	First publishers' lunch – nine hours	Columbus was Jewish, you know. Oh, yes, Jews expelled from Spain.	Mary Magdalene has twins	Clearly none of them was Jewish or he would have died much earlier.	*Bach, Mozart and Beethoven – The Movie* scheduled. Vin Diesel says, 'I'll be Beethoven,' and Arnie says, 'I'll be Bach.'

NINTENDO Japanese games company founded in 1889 by Fusajiro Yamauchi. Game Boy, Game Cube, Nintendo 64, Tetris, Super Mario Bros and their most successful product, Pokémon, are just a few of the 250 games and games systems it has so far created by this longest-selling games producer. They have to date sold over 2 billion games worldwide.

❖   ❖   ❖

These games must be good for Jewish children as they involve absolutely no physical prowess.

One game in particular, Pokémon, has not been without its share of controversy. Many see it as being part of the Zionist conspiracy. (Then again, many see the weather as being part of the Zionist conspiracy.) Judologists will be disappointed to learn that there is no evidence to back the claim that Gorönya (no. 76 in the National Pokédex) is derived from 'Golem', the clay monster – created by Rabbi Judah Ben Loew – who terrorized medieval Prague. There is, however, strong suspicion that Perrin Kaplan, currently vice-president of Nintendo US, is Jewish. Certainly sounds Jewish.

Pokémon is a Jewish threat, according to many Muslim leaders, and is banned in many Arab countries.

Some have claimed that 'Pokémon' means 'I am a Jew' in Japanese and believe the toy craze is a demonic Jewish plot to turn Arab children away from Islam. (In fact, 'Pokémon' means 'pocket monsters', which does not, at first glance, have a strong Jewish etymological link.)

A fatwa, or religious edict, has been issued by a Saudi sheikh arguing that the Pokémon cards bear 'six-pointed stars, a symbol of international Zionism and the State of Israel'. Sheikh Abdel Moneim Abu Zant, a Saudi religious figure, has declared: 'The Pokémon craze is a Jewish plot aimed at forcing our children to forgo their faith and values and to distract them from more important things such as scientific ambitions.' If you take away the phrase 'a Jewish plot', is there such a huge difference to the kind of argument exercised in many Jewish households?

Surprisingly, only one movie can be found that explores the Jews' relationship with Nintendo. The hit Swedish movie *Bit by Bit* (2002, dir. Jonathan Metzger) explores the terrible choice a young Jew must make between attending the Nintendo World Cup Games or staying with his family to celebrate Passover. Agony.

---

backlash + impact x j-factor = tzurus ÷ kabbalah = good/not good

5 + 5 x 4 = 40 ÷ 7 = 5.7

✳ **NINTENDO IS NOT GOOD FOR THE JEWS.**

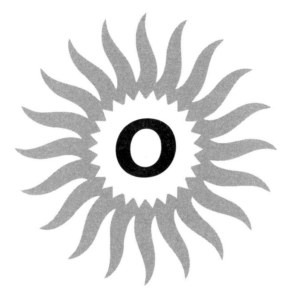

ORAL HYGIENE AND DENTISTRY Oral hygiene refers to cleanliness of the mouth, particularly teeth and gums. Keeping the mouth clean by brushing teeth, flossing and visiting the dentist is the best way to prevent tooth decay, gum disease and halitosis. The patron saint of dentists is Saint Apollonia, martyred in Alexandria by having all her teeth violently extracted. (Source: wikipedia.org.)

◆　◆　◆

How many of us have wondered why it costs so much to pay someone to inflict pain on us, terrorize our children and play such dreadful muzak while doing it? It costs around £150 to extract a tooth, an operation that takes the dentist approximately twenty seconds to perform. It seems unfair. Perhaps if they pulled more slowly, patients might feel they're getting their money's worth.

Dentistry has not always been a Jewish preserve, but it is safe to say that many luminaries in the world of oral hygiene have been Jews, for example Theodore Blum, the founder of the New York Institute of Clinical Oral Pathology, and Isaac Schour, who used teeth to study systematic disorders. A Jewish dentist was the first to use cocaine as an anaesthetic in dentistry. Alfred Einhorn, another Jew, then introduced Novocain in 1905. He was sick of the complaints from his neighbours about the snorting noises coming from his lavatories.

Famous Jewish dentists? Leach Cross (aka Dr Louis C. Wallach) was a former lightweight champion; Faye Kellerman (*Day of Atonement* and *The Ritual Bath*) is a Jewish mystery author who received a dental degree but never practised. Goldie Hawn said once all she wanted was to marry 'a Jewish dentist'. I agree, the list is pretty thin.

What sticks in my craw is when your dentist and his beautiful assistant run out of the room during a radiograph of your teeth. How reassuring it is to hear them sniggering as gamma rays are pumped into your jaw while they shtup in a bath of your dosh.

---

backlash + impact x j-factor = tzurus ÷ kabbalah = good/not good

2.5   + 2.5   x 4   = 20   ÷ 7   = 2.86

 ## ORAL HYGIENE AND DENTISTRY ARE NOT GOOD FOR THE JEWS

PDAs Personal Data Assistants, a hand-held wireless device that combines mobile phone, e-mail and GPS technology. One of the most popular PDAs is the Blackberry, rumoured to have been initially designed for Intelligence Services. It was created by Research In Motion (RIM), a Canadian company founded in 1984 by engineering students Mike Lazaridis and Douglas Fregin. The huge popularity of this device has led to accusations of users being 'Crackberry addicts' and communicating in jargon like 'Berry me, honey'.

♦   ♦   ♦

PilotYid is a company that configures Palm Pilots (PDAs) for observant Jews, so now you have no excuse to be late for the Sabbath. And if you have missed morning prayers, why not download the Tefilot (prayers) as well as portions of the Talmud and Torah for the super-zealous. It also allows downloads of local kosher restaurants (huge demand for this facility) and offers a virtual menorah for those with no time to light the lamp. Paltalk offers an internet service that provides Torah classes via videoconference, so now you can enjoy your snooze in front of the rabbi's sermon, guilt-free.

Followers of Islam are catered for by companies such as LG Electronics and the Dubai-based Ilkone Mobile

Telecommunications, which make phones that aid Muslims in their daily practice by indicating the direction of Mecca and incorporating the Qu'ran within the phone.

This is one case where technology aids religion. If Moses had been given a Blackberry, he could have been spared a second trip up Mount Sinai, had Aaron berried him with 'Come back down, the Jews have gone crazy over a cow.'

There is nothing inherently Jewish about the PDA aside from the fact that now all mothers can keep track of their sons no matter what time of day or night. Is it such a crime to stay in touch?

---

backlash + impact x j-factor = tzurus ÷ kabbalah = good/not good
4.8   + 6.1   x 5.75   = 62.67 ÷ 7   = 8.95

☀ **PDAS ARE GOOD FOR THE JEWS.**

PHYSICAL EDUCATION Also known as PE, an integral part of the school curriculum as a means to introduce exercise into children's lives. Inner-city schools are less likely to engage in field sports or cross-country running than rural schools but may engage in more gym-based activities.

◆ ◆ ◆

The clichéd picture of the bespectacled Jew in stringy vest and patterned shorts hiding wiry legs is clearly erroneous. Some say that exercise to a Jew is like salt to a slug or gefilte fish to a Goy – it is simply not meant to be. However, Jews have been successful warriors in the Bible, and in modern times the Israeli Defence Force is feared, so this school of thought is full of holes.

The Jewish reputation for shirking sports and PE is more likely to be about the shaming ritual of undressing in the boys' changing rooms. No one needs reminding that the young man was mutilated 'down there' as an infant. Also, for some Jews in areas such as, say, south-west England or anywhere in France, disclosure of ethnicity will spell an immediate beating after school.

Perhaps there is also a residual, atavistic sense of shame in undressing for exercise? According to the *Encylopedia Judaica*, a gymnasium was built by Jason in Jerusalem in 174 BC, and all the participants were obliged to perform in their birthday suits. Some of the Jewish participants, according to I Maccabees 1:15, actually underwent operations for the purpose of concealing the fact that they were circumcised. Reverse circumcision just to get into PE – these biblical Jews were all meshugge.

Some great things have happened during PE. Ben and Jerry famously met in junior high gym class in Merrick, Long Island. According to the Ben & Jerry website, 'Ben Cohen and Jerry Greenfield hated running, but they loved food. In 1978 they decided to go into business together.' The rest is history.

A by-product of the Jewish aversion to PE was the mastery of the sick note. This necessitated an over-developed medical knowledge in adolescent Jews, which in turn resulted in a high volume of Jewish doctors, thereby contributing immeasurably to general society.

---

backlash	+	impact	x j-factor	= tzurus	÷ kabbalah	= good/not good
5.8	+ 4.7	x 5.1	= 53.55 ÷ 7			= 7.65

✺ PE IS BORDERLINE AND THEREFORE NOT GOOD FOR THE JEWS.

POPE BENEDICT XVI (Born 16 April 1927 as Joseph Alois Ratzinger in Bavaria, Germany) The 265th reigning pope, the head of the Roman Catholic Church and the sovereign of the Vatican City. He was elected on 19 April 2005 and was enthroned on 7 May 2005.

When Ratzinger turned fourteen he joined the Hitler Youth. In 1943, Ratzinger was drafted into the FlaK (anti-aircraft artillery corps). In 1945, days before the German surrender, Ratzinger deserted.

♦ ♦ ♦

A Nazi pope? He joined the Hitler Youth, then the army and, during his time as Pope-in-waiting in the early eighties, he became the head of the Congregation for the Doctrine of the Faith, the new-and-improved name for the Inquisition. In his book *God and the World* (published in 2000) he says, 'We wait for the instant in which Israel will say "yes" to Christ, God and the World.' Funny, a lot of people have been waiting for that.

However, in 1936, membership of the Hitler Youth was legally required, and his time in the army did not involve fighting, and he did desert, albeit late in the day. More importantly, he worked tirelessly behind the scenes to open relations between the Vatican and Israel, and he did qualify his position on the thorny issue of Judeo-Christian relations by saying, 'The fact Jews don't accept Jesus must not be seen as an act of rejecting God, but as part of God's plan to remind the world that peace and salvation for all humanity has not yet come' (Pontifical Biblical Studies Commission, quoted in *Ha'aretz* newspaper). However, in July 2005, he pointedly omitted to name the Jews as victims of terrorist outrages when he sympathized with 'Egypt, Turkey, Iraq and Great Britain'.

His Holiness' recent visit to Auschwitz must be viewed favourably by Judologists.

However, it is important to scotch the rumour here that as a young cardinal Ratzinger's penances at Confession included 'three Heil Marys'.

---

backlash + impact x j-factor = tzurus ÷ kabbalah = good/not good
5.6   + 6.5   x 4.5   = 54.45 ÷ 7   = 7.78

POPE BENEDICT XVI IS BORDERLINE AND THEREFORE NOT GOOD FOR THE JEWS.

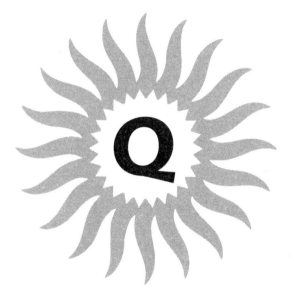

QUEENS The largest of five boroughs of New York City. In 1898 Queens, Brooklyn, the Bronx and Staten Island joined up with Manhattan. Queens and Brooklyn are part of Long Island. Queens is the largest borough, largely residential and contains a diversity of ethnic minorities. Out of the 2,229,379 residents of this borough, just under 200,000 Jews live in Queens today.

❖   ❖   ❖

Queens is a good place to die. Many famous Jews are buried in its vast networks of kosher burial grounds. According to the infinitely useful website findagrave.com, the following Jews have found peace in the quiet suburbs of Queens:

Shalom Aleichem (d. 1916), author whose stories were the basis for *Fiddler on the Roof*.

Lorenz Hart (d. 1943), lyricist who wrote the lyrics of the musical *Pal Joey* and songs such as 'The Lady is a Tramp'.

Harry Houdini, or Ehrich Weiss (d. 1926), escapologist. Still waiting for him to re-emerge.

Minnie Marx (d. 1929), mother of the Marx brothers. Of interest to students of comedy.

Alan King (d. 2004), comedian. Of no interest to students of comedy.

Edward G. Robinson, or Emmanuel Goldenberg (d. 1973), a Jew who played at being a mobster.

Louis 'Louis Cohen' Kerzner, Jacob 'Little Augie' Orgen, Abraham 'Kid Twist' Reles, Arnold Rothstein, Abraham Weinberg, Jews who did not have to play at being gangsters.

Rabbi Menachem Mendel Schneerson, 'The Rebbe' (d. 1994), not a gangster but believed by some to be the Messiah. Like Houdini, we are still waiting for his re-appearance.

Barbra Streisand (NDY – not dead yet), singer and actress. Mount Hebron Cemetery in Flushing is the location of her future burial site. Plot: section 104, near the road, in case you want visiting practice.

Queens may not be the most exciting borough in New York, but it is the most culturally and ethnically diverse. It has a fine history of Jewish residents who have distinguished themselves in the entertainment business: from Simon and Garfunkel to Joey Ramone; from Adrien Brody to Ethel Merman. But it is the fictional home of many more. Archie Bunker, Doug Hefferman, Fran Fine, George Costanza (though there is some dispute over whether one can call this character Jewish). These role models for Jews around the world are all based in Queens. Not only that, there is a sprinkling of glamour to be found in Queens. Peter Parker lived in Queens before he became Spiderman, and even a Hollywood movie was set in this desirable borough – yes, *Coming to America* (Starring Eddie Murphy, 1988) was set here, which rather says it all.

Queens is as close to Long Island as you can get. A skip and jump over the Queens/Nassau border and you are in upward-mobility heaven, Great Neck. All SJQs (Starter Jews from Queens) dream of making the move one day.

However, Great Neck is also a symbol of where Jewish aspiration can go horribly wrong. The Friedman family, exposed in *Capturing the Friedmans*, the award-winning documentary about the most dsyfunctional Jewish family on earth, lived in Great Neck. After this film was broadcast, rumours of a name-change for the town to Leap Frog were quickly scotched.

Brooklyn, which might have made a more obvious choice, was not chosen for this section because:

a) the Crown Heights riots of 1991 were not good for the Jews;
b) Brooklyn does not begin with the letter 'Q'.

---

backlash + impact x j-factor = tzurus ÷ kabbalah = good/not good
3.5   + 4.5   x 6.75   = 54   ÷ 7   = 7.71

✸ QUEENS IS BORDERLINE AND THERE-FORE NOT GOOD FOR THE JEWS.

QUIDDITCH A polo-like sport (but with broomsticks) invented for the series of seven Harry Potter novels written by J. K. Rowling. Quidditch teams consist of seven players each: one Keeper, two Beaters, three Chasers, and a Seeker. The game is played with four balls, the Quaffle, two Bludgers and the Golden Snitch. The Golden Snitch is a very small golden ball with wings, which flies around the field at very high speed. It is the Seeker's job (Harry's position) to catch it, and when they do it scores 150 points for their team and usually ends the game.

✦   ✦   ✦

Quidditch's connection to Judaism is tenuous. Despite the recurrence of the Judological super number 7 (size of team), there are some who believe the derivation of Quidditch or Kvidditch comes from *kvetsch*. Who wouldn't complain playing this hazardous game, colliding with ball-bearings in mid-air?

With so little Jewish content in the Harry Potter novels, one might suspect an agenda. Nu, what's wrong with Jews, they can't be wizards too? The only Jewish character appears to be Anthony Goldstein, prefect for Ravenclaw in the *Order of the Phoenix*. There are numerous theories, though, that argue the novels are actually Jewish texts. For example:

Hogwarts	=	a Yeshiva
Harry	=	the eternal, wandering Jew
Voldemort	=	anti-Semitism through the ages

Wizardry	=	orthodox Judaism*
Muggles	=	Goyim

Or, of course, it could just be a children's story.

---

backlash + impact x j-factor = tzurus ÷ kabbalah = good/not good
1.5   + 4.5   x 2.5   = 15   ÷ 7   = 2.14

☀ QUIDDITCH IS NOT GOOD FOR THE JEWS.

QVC 'QVC is a virtual shopping mall where customers can shop for quality merchandise twenty-four hours a day, seven days a week, 364 days a year via television, telephone or computer,' according to its website. It claims to source products from 'every continent on the globe except Antarctica'. QVC stands for Quality, Value and Convenience and was founded in 1986 by Joseph M. Segel, founder of the Franklin Mint. Its customer base is now 141 million.

✦   ✦   ✦

Surely the Jews have outgrown their reputation for being voracious shoppers? The old jokes once heard on the lawns of Jewish golf clubs – 'My wife and I always

---

* Had Harry not chosen the path to being a wizard – a good Jew – he would have happily lived out his life in the darkness of ignorance and non-wizardry (non-observance).

hold hands. If I let go, she shops'; 'My wife has a black belt in shopping'; 'My wife wants to be buried at the mall – that way she knows the children will visit' – must be a thing of the past?

Sadly, evidence shows that there is still a strong affinity between Jews and the art of shopping. HSN, the Home Shopping Network, the pioneer in the field and inspiration for QVC, did originate in Florida. There have been moves to help young Jews assuage their insatiable appetites for retail. For example, in the famous castle town of York, the council planned to build a huge shopping centre on the mass grave site of a medieval massacre of Jews in 1190. What next? A Disney store in Dachau? One way of stopping Jews shopping.

Another technique to thwart the OJS (Obsessive Jewish Shopper) was adopted by Iran in the nineteenth century. According to the travel writer J. J. Benjamin, Jews were forbidden to inspect any goods in a shop; if an item was touched, the Jewish customer was required to purchase it at any quoted price. This kind of torture is barbaric. Thank goodness the situation for Jews in Iran has vastly improved since those dark times.

Is QVC Jewish? Well, Barry Diller steered the good ship during the nineties, and Comcast, its majority shareholder today, is run by Brian Roberts (son of Ralph J.), a great Jewish philanthropist and entrepreneur. Uri Geller and Joan Rivers have sold their jewellery lines on the channel to great success, but please do not be misled: non-Jews *are* allowed to buy and sell on this service. However, things did go slightly awry in 1994 when the US Department of Justice filed a lawsuit against the company for dodgy claims over a weight-loss product. Weight-loss products on a Jewish channel! How *narish* can you be? I ask you. It's like selling a swimsuit to an Eskimo.

---

backlash + impact x j-factor = tzurus ÷ kabbalah = good/not good

4.6   + 4.5   x 6.1   = 55.51 ÷ 7   = 7.93

QVC IS BORDERLINE AND THEREFORE NOT GOOD FOR THE JEWS.

WORLD TIMELINE
(PART IV – 1750 TO 2006)

WORLD

1789	1794	1803	1848	1865	1897	1912	1923	1948	1969	1970s	1980s	1990s	2000–2006
French Revolution begins.	Whisky Rebellion erupts over liquor taxes	US purchases Louisiana from French for $15 million, doubling the size of US territory	Karl Marx writes *Communist Manifesto*	American Civil War ends	First Zionist Congress	*Titanic* sinks	*Mein Kampf* written by Adolf Hitler	Gandi murdered, leading to chaos in India	Man lands on moon	Arabs and Israelis kill each other for another decade	Reagan and Thatcher era	Bush Sr in power	Bush Sr in power
George Washington becomes president				Lincoln shot at Ford's Theatre						Scorsese, Coppola and Lucas (non-Jews) dominate American cinema	Cold War ends	Clinton and Blair era	Second war in Iraq
													Osama Bin Laden still at large

JEWISH

1789	1794	1803	1848	1865	1897	1912	1923	1948	1969	1970s	1980s	1990s	2000–2006
Great prices for weekend trips to Paris.	Jews don't drink, so no issues here.	Now that is a sweet kosher deal	*Duck Soup* is smash hit on Broadway	Pretty uncivil if you ask me	Jewish mating ritual	Jews blamed – Greenberg, Goldberg, iceberg, same difference	The musical version – *Oy, Have I Got Problems!* fails to get backers	Terrible shame, but Israel is created!	Nil (no Jews involved)	Begin and Sadat win Nobel Peace Prize	Reagan very popular with Jews until he paid his respects at Bitburg SS graveyard	Bush loses Jewish vote – he was one guy against thousands of Jewish lobbies – big no no.	God told Bush to invade Iraq, God tells Jews to vote Democrat next time
First landslide victory. Got so many votes they named the town after him				First run of *The Producers* ends						Woody Allen's *Annie Hall* beats *Star Wars* for best picture Oscar (1977)	Thatcher very popular with Jews as she put most of them in her cabinet	Cigar sales rise 1,000 per cent	At least when the Israelis bombed the Osirak nuclear reactors in 1981, they were there
											Berlin Wall crashes down and lets rabid anti-Semites back into the West	The term 'Jew Labour' coined by Peter Mandelson	Jews blamed

RHINOPLASTY A surgical procedure, usually performed to enhance the appearance of the nose. Jacques Joseph (1865–1934), born Jakob Lewin Joseph in Köningsberg, Prussia, second son of Rabbi Israel Joseph, was one of the fathers of modern plastic surgery and developed methods for aesthetic plastic surgery. He believed that the way someone looks can affect their happiness and social prospects. Such disadvantages could be relieved by the cosmetic changes afforded by rhinoplasty. (Source: wikipedia.org.)

❖   ❖   ❖

'Everybody wanted to look like a Shikseh,' said Dr Thomas D. Rees, a retired plastic surgeon (Jane Gross, *New York Times*), about those heady boom-time years of rhinoplasty in the seventies. Though the numbers have declined since then, this controversial choice of batmitzvah present is still a sore point in the Jewish community.

Could it be said that the nose job is a defining anti-Semitic act? The fact that it was pioneered by Jews whose clientele were primarily other Jews does not alleviate the seriousness of the charge of Uncle Tomism, or Uncle Hymieism as it is known in some parts.

But is there such a thing as a Jewish nose? And if not, is the nose job good or bad for the Jews? Anti-Semitic literature is full of detailed diagrams of 'the Jewish nose' (see below), and therefore to acknowledge its existence is not good for the Jews, but can its removal in surgery be seen as bad for the Jews?

CLASS IV. THE JEWISH, or Hawk Nose, is very convex, and preserves its convexity like a bow, throughout the whole length from the eyes to the tip. It is thin and sharp.

It indicates considerable Shrewdness in worldly matters; a deep Insight into character, and facility of turning that insight to profitable account.

(Source: *Notes on Noses* by George Jabet, published London, 1852.)

The 'Jewish nose' has proved an asset to some people. Barbra Streisand was famously conflicted over whether to tame her schnozzle but ultimately realized it was her trademark. Jennifer Grey, star of *Dirty Dancing* with Patrick Swayze, had no such qualms and subsequently fatally damaged her career by shaving her cartilages. By her own admission, she 'began to look like that girl out of *Dirty Dancin'*, but not quite' (Channel 5 interview, 2005). A sober warning to Jews everywhere: don't cut off your nose to spite your career.

---

backlash + impact x j-factor = tzurus ÷ kabbalah = good/not good

7   + 5   x 6   = 72   ÷ 7   = 10.3

☀ **RHINOPLASTY IS GOOD FOR THE JEWS.**

ROCK 'N' ROLL Arguably, the most influential of all musical genres, rock 'n' roll had its heyday in fifties America. It emerged as a term from the phenomenon of black artists who seemingly 'rocked' while singing gospel. It found its zenith with Elvis Presley's first recording, 'That's All right Mama', in 1954. Although it takes many forms – rhythm and blues, heavy metal, surf, gospel, Christian, punk, britpop, grunge, garage, folk and so on – it is best identified by its reliance on guitar and heavy beat.

❖   ❖   ❖

For an accurate analysis of whether rock 'n' roll is good for the Jews, one need look no further than the King of Rock, Elvis Presley. In a recent documentary, *Schmelvis: Searching for the King's Jewish Roots*, evidence is shown that Elvis is Jewish. His maternal great-great-grandmother, Nancy Tackett, née Burdine, was believed to have been Jewish. Elvis had many Jewish friends as a boy growing up in Memphis. So close to the Jewish community was he as a teenager, in fact, that he was said to have had the honour of being the 'Shabbos Goy' for Rabbi Alfred Fruchter, who lived upstairs from him. Mrs Fruchter has said that he was a 'particularly big fan of matzo ball soup and challah'. Later in life, he wore a Star of David side by side with his cross around his neck. This could have been a severe case of hedging one's bets, but let us assume it was due to his natural affinity for Jews.

However, one slip on the Judological scale must be the recording of 'Edelweiss' while serving in the US army in Germany. Not necessary.

Many of Elvis' hits were written by Jerry Leiber and Mike Stoller ('Hound Dog', 'Jailhouse Rock' and many more), and many Jews were involved in his biggest hits ('King Creole', 'Treat me Nice', 'Stuck on You', 'Good Luck Charm', 'Big Hunk o' Love', 'It's Now or Never', 'Surrender', 'Viva Las Vegas', 'Suspicion' and others).

The history of rock is peppered with Jewish influence, as the following list shows:

JEWS WHO ROCK OR THE SHUL OF ROCK

Michael Bolton (born Michael Bolotin) – OK, not a great start, but the man with the hair has sold a lot of records.

Mick Jones of the Clash – known for their progressive views on race relations, the Clash were an important punk rock band. Still, did they need to be quite so rude?

Sammy Davis Jr – cool Jew.

Neil Diamond – he wrote the song 'I'm a Believer' for the Monkees. Such a nice Jewish boy. Also wrote, 'My Name is Yussel' for his movie version of *The Jazz Singer*, which was frankly pushing it.

Phil Spector – despite describing his music as 'Wagnerian', Phil followed the Irving Berlin school of making money by producing hit Christmas albums like *A Christmas Gift to You* and *Santa Claus is Coming to Town*.

Lenny Kravitz – great friend of Michael Jackson, his seventh album was entitled *Baptism*, which does not augur well.

Beck – a Scientologist now, but we can still call him a Jew.

Lou Reed (father's name, Rabinowitz) – brought transsexuals into the mainstream. Famously no great fan of Dylan and was heard to have said about him, 'If you were at a party with him, you'd have to tell him to shut up.' Sacrilege.

Billy Joel – almost raised as a Catholic, and many confuse his ethnicity with Italian, but there should be no confusion when his choice of second wife is analysed. This troubled talent from the Bronx wed an uptown girl, all-American Christie Brinkley, who looked so blonde and non-Jewish that many realized Billy must be a Jew to want her so much.

Gene Simmons – born Chaim Witz in Israel, he found love with a blonde all-American *Playboy* model. Is there a theme here?

Barry Manilow – there is some doubt about whether Mr Manilow is, in fact, Jewish. Only joking.

Kenny G (born Kenneth Gorelich) – holds the world record for blowing an E on his sax for forty-five minutes. And people pay for this?

Kinky Friedman – his hit 'They Ain't Makin Jews Like Jesus Anymore', sung with his backing group the Texas Jewboys, is a high point in Jewish rock. Kinky ran for Texas governor under the slogan 'Kinky Friedman: Why the Hell Not?'.

Beastie Boys – *Licensed to III* is a great name for a rap album by Jews and deserved its place as rap's first US number one album in 1987.

Matisyahu – not a household name yet, but this reggae rocker is a Lubavitcher Hasid from Crown Heights and has already been profiled in *Rolling Stone* magazine, appeared on MTV and has been named by *Forward* as one of the five most influential Jews in America.

(Source: jewsrock.org.)

The phenomenon of JuMu (Jewish music and secular rock) has grown in recent years with Hip Hop Hoodios and DJ Peretz exemplifying this trend.

---

backlash + impact x j-factor = tzurus ÷ kabbalah = good/not good
4.1   + 6.6   x 5.6   = 59.9 ÷ 7   = 8.6

✹ ROCK 'N' ROLL IS GOOD FOR THE JEWS.

SCHWARZENEGGER, ARNOLD Born 1947 in Thal, Austria. After serving a mandatory year in the Austrian army, Schwarzenegger became a body-builder and subsequently left Austria for Hollywood to make his name in the movies. He was not successful until he made *Conan the Barbarian* in 1981 and then went on to star in numerous action films such as *The Last Action Hero* (1993) and the *Terminator* films (1984, 1991, 2003) and comedies such as *Twins* (1988), *Kindergarden Cop* (1990) and *Junior* (1994). He was elected Governor of California in 2003.

♦   ♦   ♦

There is some discussion about how big a Nazi Arnie's father, Gustav Schwarzenegger, really was. The Wiesenthal Centre claims there is no evidence that he was a war criminal – and that has nothing to do with the $750,000 Arnie donated to the Centre – but according to the *Los Angeles Times* (14 August 2003), Schwarzenegger Snr was indeed a member of the SA, also known as the brownshirts. He joined Hitler's henchmen quite late in the day, on 1 May 1939, about six months after Kristallnacht, so it is unlikely he joined just because of the nice uniform.

Arnie was also good friends with Kurt Waldheim, the controversial ex-Nazi former UN secretary-general and Austrian president. You can't help it if your mates just happen to be ex-Nazis (or your dad, come to that), but then I don't suppose you need to invite a high-profile war criminal to your wedding (summer 1986) and then spend most of your wedding speech extolling his great Austrian qualities (or 'kvalities').

Good ole Arnie isn't shy of courting anti-Semites. He was seen enjoying the company of Jorg Haider, the leader of the Austrian extreme right-wing Freedom Party, in 1996 and there is of course his famous comment to reporters after the release of the movie *Pumping Iron* in 1976, in which he expressed admiration for good ole Adolf: news stories quoted him as saying that he 'admired Hitler's rise to power and wished he could have experienced the thrill the Nazi leader must have had holding sway over huge audiences'. Since he became Republican governor of California, he has strangely dropped his Hitler impressions and courting of extremists. In fact, he helped launch plans for a Museum of Tolerance in Jerusalem and is very popular with Jews in California.

---

backlash + impact x j-factor = tzurus ÷ kabbalah = good/not good
4.6   + 3.7   x 3.6   = 29.9 ÷ 7   = 4.3

 # ARNOLD SCHWARZENEGGER IS NOT GOOD FOR THE JEWS.

SCIENTOLOGY, THE CHURCH OF Scientology was first developed in the United States in the 1950s by the author of *Dianetics*, L. Ron Hubbard (1922–86). Hubbard was virulently opposed to all forms of psychotherapy and designed Scientology as an alternative which would help humans develop their spirit through counselling (known as 'auditing') and rehabilitation. Scientology maintains that humans are spiritual beings (know as 'thetan') who have lived through many past lives and will continue to live after the death of our bodies. The Church promises to help teach people how to achieve the ultimate goal of getting the thetan back to its original state of freedom. The more advanced teachings are kept strictly confidential from new initiates and reserved for those who are 'spiritually prepared'. To this day, there continues to be some controversy over whether it is a religion or not.

✦   ✦   ✦

Scientology does have a litigious reputation, and Jon Stewart's popular *Daily Show* is rumoured to have a 'no Scientology jokes' policy because of this. A religion that can't laugh at itself is, well, frankly, not Jewish.

Scientology has had harsh critics in its short life – none

more so than the German government. Claudia Nolte, the minister of family policy, described the church as 'one of the most aggressive groups in our society'.

L. Ron Hubbard had some, shall we say, 'old-fashioned' views on race relations, and his negative stance on psychotherapy remains controversial. In 2005 Tom Cruise had a very public spat with Brooke Shields over her post-natal blues. This 'debate' about whether Ms Shields should or should not have used anti-depressants did not garner positive PR on behalf of the multi-million dollar religion. However, any movement that provides a cheaper alternative to shrink fees can't be all bad.

---

backlash + impact x j-factor = tzurus ÷ kabbalah = good/not good
3.05   + 4.15   x 1   = 7.2   ÷ 7   = 1.03

 SCIENTOLOGY IS NOT GOOD FOR THE JEWS.

SIX DEGREES OF SEPARATION A parlour game where you can connect any famous person by six stages to you or someone equally obscure or incongruous. For example, finding six links from the Pope to the Chief Rabbi of Israel. Two versions of this game are provided here for Judologists. Both are circular (starting with someone famous and coming full circle back to that person by the end), but feel free to insert your own destination point. The game was developed into Six Degrees of Kevin Bacon after it was discovered that he has appeared in so many movies that he can be connected to every actor on Earth.

Six Degrees of Larry David* (using Jews only)

1) Larry David appeared in a cameo role in *Radio Days*, a movie by Woody Allen.
2) Woody Allen learned his craft in the fifties with top comic Sid Caesar.
3) Sid Caesar discovered Mel Brooks on his *Show of Shows*.
4) Mel Brooks cast Zero Mostel in the first movie version of *The Producers*.
5) Zero Mostel's character, Max Bialystock, was played in the theatrical production by Jason Alexander.
6) Jason Alexander played George Costanza in *Seinfeld*, a character based on Larry David.

Judologists prefer Seven Degrees, as the number 7 is more spiritual. The rules of this version are less stringent here, and non-Jews can be used in this game. For example:

Seven Degrees of Woody Allen

1) Woody Allen's muse in his recent movies is Scarlett Johansson.
2) Scarlett Johansson's early movie *Eight Legged Freaks* starred David Arquette.

---

* Apologies to Kevin Bacon, who, for obvious reasons, could not be part of this game.

3) David Arquette is married to Courtney Cox, star of *Scream* and *Friends*.
4) Courtney Cox sprang to fame after being pulled from a crowd by Bruce Springsteen in his video of 'Dancing in the Dark'.
5) Bruce Springsteen wrote the song 'Shut out the Light' for the movie *Born on the Fourth of July*, starring Tom Cruise
6) Tom Cruise had a row about Scientology with Scarlett Johansson, forcing her to pull out of *Mission Impossible III*.
7) Scarlett Johansson is the new muse of Woody Allen.

Please feel free to play this at home using other famous Jewish and Gentile names. I would like to suggest the following for beginners:

Dov Ber Borochov, pioneer of early Zionism: six degrees to Peter André.
The Baal Shem Tov, founder of Chasidism: six degrees to Britney Spears.
God, Prime Mover and Creator of Everything: six degrees to Louis Walsh. Only joking, that would be impossible. Try Jon Snow.

Oodles of fun for the Judologist on a break from his or her calculations.

STAR TREK Gene Roddenberry created this huge television, publishing and movie franchise. The original *Star Trek* TV series aired between 1966 and 1969 on NBC. Although spin-off series were developed in the nineties, it is the original three TV series with their eighty episodes that remain most popular. The show depicts the journeys on the USS *Enterprise*, whose mission is to 'boldly go where no man has gone before' and seek out new civilizations while promoting peace and understanding throughout the galaxy.

◆　　◆　　◆

Though created by a non-Jew, *Star Trek* eerily contains many Jewish components and themes. Aside from the obvious – USS *Enterprise* is hardly the name of a non-Jewish space ship is it? – several key cast members were Jewish. William Shatner (Captain Kirk), Leonard Nimoy (Spock) and Walter Koenig (Chekhov) were all Jews. Spock's Vulcan greeting was invented by Leonard Nimoy and was based on his memories of shul, when he was asked to perform the ritual blessing of the Kohanim (the priests) and learned the secret sign. (Some Trekkies believe that *The Wrath of Khan*, the movie, had its title changed by Nimoy from *The Wrath of Kohen*.) Other obvious parallels between Vulcans and Jews: big ears instead of big noses; great powers of assimilation though outsiders (aliens, in fact); both peoples are very brainy and good at chess.

Spock was, of course, only half Vulcan – his father was Vulcan and mother was human. Unlike Orthodox Jewish culture, Vulcan culture is not strictly matrilineal, and Spock considered himself Vulcan even though his mother wasn't one. There is no evidence as to whether Spock had trouble getting his children into the best Vulcan schools (there is a long waiting list for VFS – Vulcan Free School) as a result of this, but there is considerable proof to support the argument that Spock's parents were not frum Vulcans.

The one strange anomaly in this argument is that the doctor, Bones McCoy, was not Jewish. Whoever heard of a non-Jewish doctor?

---

backlash	+ impact	x j-factor	= tzurus	÷ kabbalah	= good/not good
4	+ 6	x 6	= 60	÷ 7	= 8.57

✳ *STAR TREK* **IS GOOD FOR THE JEWS.**

STAR WARS Film directed by George Lucas and released in 1977 and also the generic name for the cycle of films (two sequels and three prequels), which culminated in 2005 with *The Revenge of the Sith*. A classic reworking of the good versus evil storyline as a futuristic inter-galactic epic, *Star Wars* tells of the struggle between the Rebel Alliance and the Galactic Empire thousands of years into the future. The protagonist of the first movie is the young Luke Skywalker, who leaves his home planet, teams up with other rebels and tries to save Princess Leia, who is being held captive by the evil Darth Vader. *Star Wars* was, at the time, the biggest-grossing movie of all time.

✦   ✦   ✦

Lucas is neither Jewish nor German, but the Jewish references are many. For 'Galactic Empire' read 'Weimar Republic'; a chancellor issuing emergency decrees and pronouncing himself emperor forever rings a faint bell with those who remember a certain historical figure in the first half of the twentieth century; even more subtle is the name of the emperor's personal guard – Stormtroopers; both emperors lose wars, and eventually the dicatorships they turned their empires into become republics again; and to round it off, we have segregated parts of Coruscant for all non-human species, which are nothing at all like ghettos for *Untermenschen*.

However, certain *Star Wars* commentators have expressed concern over the character Watto the Toydarian. A slave trader with a hideous hooked nose, strong shtetlized East European accent and abominable teeth bent on destroying the beautiful blond Annakin – might he be seen as an anti-Semitic stereotype. Other experts argue the contrary and provide proof that *Star Wars* is in fact a Jewish text. Obi-wan Kenobi is also known as Ben Kenobi. 'A navi' is a prophet in Hebrew – ahem, isn't that his role?

But the slam-dunk on this issue must be the first scene in *Star Wars*, when C3PO and R2D2 are wandering (get the reference?) on Tatooine. C3PO bemoans his fate: 'We seem to be made to suffer. That's our lot in life.' Surely, Jewish robots.

---

backlash + impact x j-factor = tzurus ÷ kabbalah = good/not good

5.5　　+ 5.1　 x 6.1　　= 64.66 ÷ 7　　 = 9.24

 STAR WARS IS GOOD FOR THE JEWS.

STILLER, BEN (Born 1965 in New York) Hollywood actor/director, best known for comedy roles in *Zoolander* (2001), which he wrote and directed, *Reality Bites* (1994), which he also directed, *There's Something About Mary* (1998), *Meet the Parents* (2000) and *Meet the Fockers* (2004).

♦　♦　♦

Hollywood's rent-a-Jew? Gaylord 'Greg' Focker in *Meet the Parents* and *Meet the Fockers*, Reuben Feffer in *Along Came Polly* and Rabbi Jake Schram in *Keeping the Faith*. Even when not specifically Jewish, he is always Jewish – for example, *Reality Bites, The Royal Tennenbaums* and *There's Something About Mary*. He has managed to convey the Jew on screen as fractionally less nerdy (he works out) and not as irritating as Ross in *Friends* or Woody Allen in any of his last seven movies.

His father is Jerry Stiller, who often appeared in *Seinfeld* and had a popular comedy double act with his wife, Anne Meara (Miranda's mother-in-law in *Sex and the City*). He played the funny Jewish guy and she his Irish bride. Which was true. She was born Catholic but converted to Judaism six years after marrying Jerry.

Despite his success and his overt Jewishness, people still like him. Even in the Midwest, where they don't like Jews, they do like Ben Stiller – *Zoolander* did extremely well at the box office there. But Stiller does have his critics. David Denby wrote in the *New Yorker*, 'Stiller is the latest, and crudest, version of the urban Jewish male on the make.' He has been labelled the Paul Michael Glaser of the noughties, but a Jew who doesn't have to look like Paul Newman or Kirk Douglas playing the lead is a step in the right direction, no?

Perhaps Stiller's marriage to a model who is both blonde and called Christine causes Jews to feel conflicted. Between jealousy and envy. In fact, several of Stiller's characters go for blondes, like Teri Polo in *Meet the Parents*, or Jennifer Elfman in *Keeping the Faith* and a blondish Jennifer Aniston in *Polly*, where Jewish alternative girlfriends are dumped in favour of all-American non-Jewesses. When he did fall for a Jewish leading lady in *Reality Bites* – Winona Ryder (Horowitz) – the movie received only cult status. The pursuit of the Shiksa is one of the great Hollywood themes and has nothing to do with unhappily married Jewish movie executives acting out their fantasies.

---

backlash + impact x j-factor = tzurus ÷ kabbalah = good/not good

5   + 5   x 7   = 70 ÷ 7   = 10

 BEN STILLER IS GOOD FOR THE JEWS.

SUDOKU A number puzzle consisting of a 9 x 9 grid split into 3 x 3 sub-grids. Each row, column and 3 x 3 box must contain the numbers 1–9. Sudoku puzzles appear with a few numbers already filled in – the puzzle solver must use these to work out where all the other numbers go.

This type of puzzle was first created by Leonhard Euler, a Swiss mathematician, in 1776. In 1984, the leading puzzle company in Japan, Nikoli, discovered the puzzles and began publishing them under the name Suuji Wa Dokushin Ni Kagiru, which means 'the numbers must occur only once'. They became very popular, among the best-selling puzzles in Japan, and in 1986 the president of Nikoli shortened the name to Sudoku (*su* means number and *doku* means single).

◆   ◆   ◆

The Sudoku virus hit the West in November 2004, when *The Times* printed their first puzzle. It spread to New York in April 2005, when the *New York Post* adopted it, followed by *USA Today*, spurring over 100 international bestselling books.

Why is Sudoku good for the Jews? Aside from sounding like Tzedakah, any puzzle that uses numbers is good for the Judologist (although a slight disappointment must be expressed that 9 is the chosen number and not 7). Some shame and slight embarrassment must be expressed that no Jewish links can be made to the creation of this numerical craze. However, Jews should be good at number games.* They have enough experience of charging by the hour. It is no accident that the fourth book of Moses is called Numbers.

As we know, Gematriya (numerical value of Hebrew letters) is a central plank of Talmudic learning and therefore should prove good training to Sudokists. According to Jeremy Maissel of the *Jerusalem Post*, if you put 'Sudoku itself to the gematriya test, Sudoku totals 182, the equivalent of *holech vehazek* – getting stronger and stronger – which characterizes the popularity of the new craze and reassuringly confirms the authentic significance of gematriya.' Wise words.

Downside? To make room for Sudoku, newspapers are shedding their bridge columns, which is catastrophic for the Jews of Bournemouth.

*Plans to bring out the Institute's own version, Judoku, have been temporarily delayed due to a severe lack of demand, but a book of puzzles should be ready for press in time for the Christmas '07 market.

---

backlash + impact x j-factor = tzurus ÷ kabbalah = good/not good
3.4   + 6.6   x 6.2   = 62   ÷ 7   = 8.85

☀ **SUDOKU IS GOOD FOR THE JEWS.**

TATTOOS The word tattoo is derived from the Tahitian *tatu*, which means 'to mark something'. The earliest identified tattoos are from Ancient Egypt, though it has been claimed that tattooing has existed since 12,000 years BC. Tattoos are more popular now than at any time in recorded history.

✦   ✦   ✦

The Old Testament tells us that tattoos are bad for the Jews. Hidden away in the book of Leviticus, snuggled neatly after the legal quagmire of cross-breeding animals, lies this decree: 'Ye shall not make any cuttings in your flesh for the dead, nor print any marks upon you' (Leviticus 19:28). Maimonides, the great scholar, took a dim view of tattooing, saying it was a pretty pagan thing to do: 'this was the custom of the Gentiles that they inscribe themselves for idol worship'. Despite the fact that the myth that Jews with tattoos will not be buried in a Jewish cemetery has been dispelled, why do so many Jews love to defile themselves so?

Perhaps the greatest living Jewish advocate of the ancient art is David Beckham. The former England captain has nine tattoos. In November 2000, he had tattooed the name of his wife – former Spice Girl Victoria Beckham – written in Hindi. Beckham was soon to learn that the artist had in fact spelled out 'Vihctoria'. Not quite as bad as JFK's gaffe 'Ich bin ein Berliner' (translation: I am a jam doughnut), but a pretty strong contender. Seemingly unconcerned about his lack of talent with languages, he followed this with a Latin phrase on his left forearm and, most recently, a phrase in Hebrew from Shir Hashirim (Song of Songs). 'I am for my beloved and my beloved is for me' is what he thinks it says. 'Don't fancy yours much, mate' is a closer translation. Women with tattoos have traditionally been highly attractive to Jewish men. After all, they must be experienced in making decisions they regret later.

---

backlash + impact x j-factor = tzurus ÷ kabbalah = good/not good

$$2 + 2 \times 2 = 8 \div 7 = 1.14$$

☀ TATTOOS ARE NOT GOOD FOR THE JEWS.

TIVO OR SKYPLUS A popular brand of digital video recorder that allows users to store television programming to an internal hard drive for later viewing. One of its most popular features is the selection of the programming based on the user's past preferences. Additionally, programmes being watched 'live' can be paused or 'rewound' to repeat a sequence just watched.

* * *

This simple device has revolutionized the lives of millions of Jews around the world. Only now can you pause a live game on TV to finish that raging argument with your spouse or children and not ruin the enjoyment of live sport. Also, crucially, the male of the house is able to fast forward all commercial breaks, saving himself thousands of pounds in domestic products that his wife now cannot see. In religious or observant Jewish families, the SkyPlus is known affectionately as the 'Shabbos Goy' (traditionally, local non-Jews were employed to use electrical goods, as Jews were prohibited from doing so under the laws of the Sabbath).

A man called his rabbi and said, 'I know tonight is Kol Nidre, the holiest night in the Jewish calendar, but Spurs are playing their fourth-round replay with Man U. Rabbi, I've got to watch the Spurs game on TV.' 'Aha,' the Rabbi responds, 'That's what SkyPlus is for.' The man was impressed. 'You mean I can record Kol Nidre?'

Possibly the most compelling argument why this magical recorder is good for the Jews must lie in its 'season pass manager' facility. This allows the viewer to pick an automatic function that records all the series of any particular show by one hit of the button. By simply looking in the documentaries section and selecting 'documentaries', you can have all possible programmes on the Second World War recorded for you at any time of day or night. Unfortunately, there is no ability yet to programme 'Jew only' commands.

SkyPlus and TiVo are the ultimate tools for the serious Judologist.

---

backlash + impact x j-factor = tzurus ÷ kabbalah = good/not good

3.45 + 5.2 x 6.66 = 57.61 ÷ 7 = 8.23

 TiVO/SKYPLUS IS GOOD FOR THE JEWS.

TRIAL OF MICHAEL JACKSON, THE Born
Michael Joseph Jackson on 29 August 1958 in Gary, Indiana, the 'King of Pop' was performing by the age of six as the lead singer and youngest member of the Jackson Five. He began his solo career in 1979 with the album *Off the Wall* and achieved global fame with his 1982 album *Thriller*. The June 2005 trial began as a result of the broadcast of a documentary, *Living with Michael Jackson*, on ABC, presented by Brit journalist Martin Bashir, who got Mr Jackson to admit to sharing his bed with boys. One of those boys, Gavin Arvizo, a recovering cancer patient, claimed that Mr Jackson had showed him pornography and plied him with alcohol. Mr Jackson was arrested and indicted on ten counts including lewd acts on a child and supplying alcohol to a minor. Michael Jackson was cleared of all charges.

◆ ◆ ◆

Michael Jackson is not shy when it comes to expressing his feelings about Jews. *Good Morning America* aired (November 2005) a two-year-old answering-machine message on which Mr Jackson was seemingly heard to rant on about Jews as 'leeches' and being part of a 'conspiracy'. Mind you, this is from the great lyricist whose 1995 hit 'They Don't Care About Us' included the wonderful rhyme 'Jew Me, Sue Me' before it was removed following protests from the Anti-Defamation League.

Surprising, then, to discover that so many Jews have been employed by him and have leapt to his side during times of trouble. Benjamin Brafman was part of his defence team (he is best known for winning an acquittal in 2001 for Sean 'P. Diddy' Combs on bribery and weapons charges). The actor Corey Feldman, Rabbi Shmuley Boteach and Uri Geller all supported him before the trial.

Concern must be raised over his choice of hotel where his entourage stayed during the trial. The Chumash Casino, where MJ also held his victory celebration after being cleared of the charges, does sound pretty Jewish, but Chumash is actually the name of the local Indian tribe that runs the casino rather than the five books of the Torah, but no smoke without fire, etc. There were rumours that the notoriously anti-Semitic Nation of Islam would be playing a significant role in MJ's affairs, but this has been denied by the Nation spokespeople. In fact, they were insulted by the slur.

---

backlash + impact x j-factor = tzurus ÷ kabbalah = good/not good

3　　　+ 5　　x 4.5　 = 36　 ÷ 7　　　 = 5.1

THE MICHAEL JACKSON TRIAL IS NOT GOOD FOR THE JEWS.

USA PATRIOT ACT, THE Passed by the US Congress in the aftermath of 9/11 in October 2001, it grants the Federal Government increased power to access private records, conduct secret searches and detain and deport non-citizens. Highly controversial, this Act was rushed through Congress with little time for public debate or discussion.

❖   ❖   ❖

USA PATRIOT stands for 'Uniting and Strengthening America by Providing Appropriate Tools Required to Intercept and Obstruct Terrorism'. Also known as, 'Unless Somebody Asks, People Are Treasonous Rogues Intent on Terror'.

Jews tend to be split on this issue. On the one hand, Jews have always been at the forefront of the war against infringements of civil liberties, but this law could be said to protect Jews from attacks in places where Jews congregate in large numbers, such as temples, community centres and shopping malls. Besides, when was snooping on your neighbour a criminal offence? Without gossip and rumour, even fewer Jews would attend synagogue during the high holy days.

As nobody has really read the whole Act, nobody

really knows how much of it is simply uncontroversial updates to pre-existing privacy laws in response to technological change and how much of it empowers an opportunistic administration bent on crushing all civil liberties to usher in a new McCarthy era.

By far the most compelling argument for the PATRIOT Act comes from Rabbi David Feldman, a spokesperson for Jews Against Anti-Semitism. He states, 'Under Section 802 of the 2001 USA PATRIOT Act, any crime which endangers human life is defined as an act of domestic terrorism. Mel Gibson's incitement of anti-Semitism is a civil disobedience crime which endangers human life under the PATRIOT Act. His creation of the movie *The Passion of the Christ* is an act of domestic terrorism.' Who could argue with that?

---

backlash + impact x j-factor = tzurus ÷ kabbalah = good/not good

7   + 5   x 1   = 12   ÷ 7   = 1.7

☀ THE USA PATRIOT ACT IS NOT GOOD FOR THE JEWS.

V

VACATION SPOTS

A checklist for the travelling Judologist who is unsure about spending his/her money in countries that do not welcome him/her. Please note that all distances are calculated from the Judological Institute's international headquarters in Cockfosters, Hertfordshire.

New Zealand

- Jewish population: 5,000.
- Distance from Cockfosters, UK: 11,390 miles (18,329 km) (9,898 nautical miles).
- J-factor: New Zealand has had two Jewish prime ministers. Julius Vogel was prime minister from 1873 to 1875 and then again in 1876; he was famous for his support of women's suffrage, which led to New Zealand being the first country in the world to give women the vote in 1893. The second was Francis Bell, though he was only officially prime minister for sixteen days in 1925, when Prime Minister William Massey died. His mother was Jewish. New Zealand did vote in the UN in favour of the creation of the state of Israel in 1948.

- Drawback: not much to do when you get there other than extreme sports, clearly not good for the Jews.

New Zealand is a good vacation spot for the Jews.

Malaysia

- Jewish population: 0.
- Distance from Cockfosters, UK: 6,557 miles (10,552 km) (5,698 nautical miles).
- J-factor: other than the fact that Israelis are not allowed into the country, back in October 2003, the country's prime minister, Mahathir Mohamad, addressed the Tenth Islamic Summit Conference with these immortal words:

The Muslims will forever be oppressed and dominated by the Europeans and the Jews . . . 1.3 billion Muslims cannot be defeated by a few million Jews . . . The Europeans killed 6 million Jews out of 12 million. But today the Jews rule this world by proxy. They get others to fight and die for them . . . We are up against a people who think. They survived 2,000 years of pogroms not by hitting back, but by thinking. They invented and successfully promoted Socialism, Communism, human rights and democracy so that persecuting them would appear to be wrong, so they may enjoy equal rights with others. With these they have now gained control of the most powerful countries, and they, this tiny community, have become a world power . . . They are already beginning to make mistakes. And they will make more mistakes. There may be windows of opportunity for us now and in the future. We must seize these opportunities.

Malaysia is not a good vacation spot for Jews.

Guyana

- Jewish population: about 10.
- Distance from Cockfosters, UK: 4,523 miles (7,279 km) (3,931 nautical miles).
- J-factor: Guyana had a Jewish president from 1997 to 1999: Janet Jagan, born Janet Rosenberg in Chicago in 1920. She was the first white president of Guyana, the first elected female president in South America and the first Jewish head of state in South American history. Her son is now entering politics, so there could be another one.
- Drawback: no kosher restaurants.

Guyana is a good vacation spot for the Jews.

Monaco

- Jewish population: Monaco has more Jews per capita than anywhere else in the world bar Israel at 30.85 in 1,000 people.
- Distance from Cockfosters, UK: 651 miles (1,048 km) (566 nautical miles).
- J-factor: Jews love a good spiel, so why not go out in style?

Monaco is a good vacation spot for the Jews.

Iceland

- Jewish population: 12 or so.
- Distance from Cockfosters, UK: 1,177 miles (1,894 km) (1,023 nautical miles).
- J-factor: despite having the smallest self-styled Jewish community in the world, Iceland's first lady is Israeli-born Dorrit Moussaieff, which is quite a feat. With such a small community, why not pop over? After all, you never call . . . The community meets for a seder, as well as for Rosh Hashanah and Hanukkah, so now there's no excuse. And yes, Iceland did vote in favour of the creation of the Jewish state.

Iceland is a good vacation spot for the Jews.

Kentucky, USA

- Jewish population: 12,000.
- Distance from Cockfosters UK: 3,723 miles (5,991 km) (3,235 nautical miles).
- J-factor: Kentucky's Southern hospitality has not always extended to those of the Hebraic persuasion. In 1862 General Ulysses S. Grant issued an order expelling the Jews from Kentucky for apparently violating trade regulations. (OK, Abe Lincoln ordered him to revoke it three days later, but still . . .) Despite the Jewish mayor of Louisville (Jerry Abramson), Kentucky is still not a great place for the wandering Judologist. There is an ongoing 'debate' about the Christian Right's desire to post the Ten

Commandments on every civic building and public school. Some, like State Senator Albert Robinson, believe the term 'Judeo-Christian' is oppressive to Christians, and we should remember that '"When the boat came to these great shores, it did not have an atheist, a Buddhist, a Hindu, a Muslim, a Christian and a Jew. Ninety-eight-plus per cent of these people were Christians"' (source: religioustolerance.org). It doesn't make you want to rush into putting your kids' names on waiting lists in this state.

- Also, avoid this state in May, for that's when the good ole Nordic Fest takes place – it's a music festival which is a kind of Woodstock for white supremacists, featuring bands like Race War, Black Shirts, Totenkopf Saints and Blood and Iron. This 'Newport for the New Right' is run by the Imperial Klans of America (IKA), which believes:

> The Imperial Klans of America, Knights of the Ku Klux Klan is a law-abiding organization . . . We must protect our race, nation and our great beliefs in Christ . . . The IKA hates: muds, spics, kikes and niggers. This is our God-given right! In no way do we advocate violence. We believe in educating our people to the monopolistic Jewish control of the world's banks, governments and media.

Who could possibly complain about an organization devoted to education?

Kentucky is not a good vacation spot for the Jews.

Japan

- Jewish population: 2,000.
- Distance from Cockfosters, UK: 5,956 miles (9,585 km) (5,175 nautical miles).
- J-factor: for a country with so few Jews, there is an impressive amount of anti-Semitic material available to the casual reader, and it sells rather well. *The Protocols of the Elders of Zion*, *The International Jew* and *Mein Kampf* all became available in Japanese in the 1920s and 1930s and are published in new editions about every ten years. The main thrust of the anti-Semitism is that the Jews' prime concern is world domination as influenced by the *Protocols*. 'Jews' is sometimes used as a generic term for 'the West'. However, this is sophistry. What Jew really enjoys uncooked fish? It's not natural.

Japan is not a good vacation spot for the Jews.

Micronesia

(Four states: Pohnpei, Yap, Chuuk and Kosrae, in the Pacific Ocean somewhere between Hawaii and Indonesia)

- Jewish population: there were two Baptists in the process of converting to Judaism there but they've now made aliyah . . . so none.
- Distance from Cockfosters, UK: 8,208 miles (13,209 km) (7,133 nautical miles).

- J-factor: Micronesia scores very high on this. Inexplicably, it has developed such a relationship with Israel that it always votes for Israel at the United Nations. So much so that Yasser Arafat once dubbed Israel 'Greater Micronesia'. An American Baptist couple, Jim Bramblett and Deborah Greenhill, symbolized this strange link to the Zionist homeland. They lived in Micronesia in a completely kosher house, complete with a mikveh and beit midrash, on a hill known as Mount Zion by locals. They converted to Judaism in Honolulu and now live in Israel but while they were in Micronesia they claim they influenced their government's pro-Israel decisions on such issues as West Bank settlements, nuclear capability and Palestinian refugees by using the Old Testament to show Micronesian officials that they would be tempting divine retribution if they failed to side with Israel.

Micronesia is a good vacation spot for the Jews.
(Source: *Forward*, 6 July 2001.)

Thailand

- Jewish population: 200.
- Distance from Cockfosters, UK: 6,143 miles (9,886 km) (5,339 nautical miles).
- J-factor: there are so many Israelis in Thailand (about 50,000 visit each year) that some Thai people working in the tourist areas can actually speak Hebrew. You can visit a kosher restaurant in Bangkok and go for a Friday-night meal on Koh

Samui, and, if Buddhist temples aren't fulfilling your spiritual needs, Chabad House on the Khao San Road in Bangkok is the place to go for services on Shabbos and festivals – and they even host a free seder night.

Thailand is a good vacation spot for the Jews.

France

- Jewish population: 600,000.
- Distance from Cockfosters, UK: 213 miles (343 km) (185 nautical miles).
- J-factor: a controversial entry, what with its history of anti-Semitism – Dreyfus, the Vichy government, the recent banning of religious headwear, Le Pen and 600 anti-Semitic attacks having taken place in 2004 alone – but what great food. For Jews, food must be high on the agenda for vacation and it's madness to ignore the best culinary delights in the world for mere principles.
- The French government does tend to turn a blind eye to events such as the fire-bombing of synagogues (Lyon, Strasbourg, Marseilles), the Molotov cocktails thrown into a Jewish sports centre (Toulouse), the gunman who opened fire in a kosher butcher (Toulouse), the numerous desecrations of graveyards and regular defacing of the statue of Dreyfus (Paris), etc. The French ambassador to the United Kingdom was heard saying at a dinner party in London that the world's prob-

lems were due to 'that shitty little country, Israel'. President Jacques Chirac proudly scolded a Jewish newspaper editor in January 2005 with the statement that 'there is no anti-Semitism in this country'.

* It's not all Jew-baiting, though (serious Judologists note that France did vote for the creation of the state of Israel). France did ban the Hizbollah TV station al-Manar for incitement of anti-Semitism, and also has the largest Jewish population in Europe and the third-largest in the world, so a show of solidarity would not be out of place. Perhaps the strongest argument to support La Belle France must be its unstinting, unswerving and unbelievable support of Israel – no other country has voted as consistently highly for Israel in the Eurovision Song Contest.

France is borderline and therefore not a good vacation spot for the Jews.

Turkmenistan

* Jewish population: 1,500–2,000.
* Distance from Cockfosters, UK: don't bother.
* J-factor: President Saparmyrat Niyazov has made himself president for life and rules this state as an absolute dictator. So much so that he has even named a yoghurt after himself. He has banned ballet, opera and even the circus. Only two religions are tolerated, Russian Orthodoxy and Sunni

Islam. Aside from showing support to the perse-
cuted Jews in this darkest backwater of the old
Soviet empire, *avoid this place.*

Turkmenistan is not a good vacation spot for the Jews.

Venezuela

- Jewish population: 35,000.
- Distance from Cockfosters, UK: 4,662 miles
  (7,503 km) (4,052 nautical miles).
- J-factor: according to a report from the Stephen Roth
  Institute in Tel Aviv University, 'In Latin America,
  and particularly in Venezuela, politicians and high-
  ranking officials openly express anti-Semitic views.'
  Apparently, during the presidency of Hugo Chavez,
  the intelligence forces of the Venezuelan police raided
  a Jewish elementary and high school in the Hebraica
  Cultural and Sports Club, allegedly in search of arms.
  The 1,500 children were accused of stashing guns
  and of being behind the assassination of Federal
  Prosecutor Danilo Anderson. Perhaps the after-
  school club there is called Mini Mossad? In May
  2004, Venezuelan state radio claimed that Jews were
  disloyal to Venezuela.

Venezuela is not a good vacation spot for the Jews.

Bahrain

- Jewish population: about 30.
- Distance from Cockfosters: 3,164 miles (5,092
  km) (2,750 nautical miles).

- J-factor: Of all the Arab states Bahrain is interesting because of its ambiguous stance towards Israel and the Jews. Aside from Egypt and Jordan, which are at peace with Israel, most other Arab nations will not allow a Jew across their borders if they have the stamp of Israel on their passports. Bahrain, however, has entertained peace talks with Israel, and Bahraini Jews and Bahrainis enjoy semi-normal relationships. Before the creation of Israel in 1948, 600 Jews lived in Bahrain. Today only thirty Jews live in Bahrain, but the Jewish community is on the rise and is tolerated. Even the US State Department released a report complimenting Bahrain's policy of religious tolerance. The report, which examined religious tolerance throughout the world, noted that Bahrain's constitution provided for freedom of worship for both Muslims and non-Muslims. It may not be Miami Beach, but if you want to dip your toe in the Arab world, this Gulf state might be the place to start.

Bahrain is a good vacation spot for the Jews.

Honduras

- Jewish Population: about 200.
- Distance from Cockfosters, UK: 5,342 miles (8,597 km) (4,642 nautical miles).
- J-factor: despite abstaining in the UN vote over the creation of the state of Israel, Honduras has had two

Jewish presidents: Juan Lindo (president 1847–52) and Ricardo Maduro (born 20 April 1946 in Panama), who became president in 2002 despite a constitutional ban on non-Honduran-born presidents. Other than Marranos (descendants of the Jews who were expelled from Spain in 1492 and practised in secret), who came to Honduras and assimilated completely, Jews first arrived at the end of the nineteenth century and were welcomed to the country until 1936, when immigration was halted. In the last fifteen years there has been a resurgence of Jewish life: there is a private Jewish cemetery as well as a burial society. Shul membership fees are very reasonable, so it's well worth contemplating a share in a condo here.

Honduras is a good vacation spot for the Jews.

The English Countryside

- Jewish Population: 270,000.
- Distance from Cockfosters: Just take the M25, M1 and M6 and you are roughly there.
- J-factor: The media, including the world-famous BBC, have often been criticized by Jews as being anti-Israel, but on the whole good old-fashioned anti-Semitism exists in such a polite form that international Judologists (especially our American friends) should not be put off seeing the country that, in 2006, celebrated 350 years of continual Jewish presence.

- The British Jewish community boasts the world's oldest Jewish newspaper, *The Jewish Chronicle*, founded in 1841, and provides an invaluable service to British Jews, with its famous classifieds section providing weekly lists of the dead, the born and the married. It is a wonderful reminder of who you have fallen out with and why.

The English countryside is a good vacation spot for the Jews.

Kazakhstan

- Jewish population: 15–20,000.
- Distance from Cockfosters, UK: 2,615 miles (4,209 km) (2,262 nautical miles).
- J-factor: The Soviet Republic has a questionable reputation when it comes to anti-Semitism and this is partly due to the activities of Borat Sagdiyev, the fictional creation of comic actor Sacha Baron Cohen. The Kazakh government threatened the actor with a legal suit in 2005 because it found his portrayal of Kazakhs derogatory and inflammatory. In fact, so angry were the Kazakhs about some of the inaccuracies in Mr Baron Cohen's depiction of their country, the government took out a four-page advert in the *New York Times* to argue that:

1) the national drink is, in fact, kumiss (horse milk) and not horse piss, as claimed by Cohen's alter ego, Borat;

2) most women are not kept in cages;
3) there is no evidence of a Kazakh folk song called 'Throw Jews Down A Well'.

Borat has distanced himself from Mr Baron Cohen, declaring on his website, www.borat.tv, 'I fully support my government's position to sue the Jew.' He goes further, adding that 'Kazakhstan is as civilized as any other country in the world. Women can now travel on inside of bus, homosexuals no longer have to wear blue hat and age of consent has been raised to 8 years old.'

- Kazakhstan enjoys an integrated ethnic population and has a cordial relationship with Israel (in fact, in 2004 more than $300 million was invested in the country from Israel). Be aware, though, of the 'orteke' dance as it enacts the pain felt by a goat falling into a hole. Don't laugh when you see this in a Kazakhstani tavern, as this is a cultural tradition.
- Oh, yes. Kazakhstan is one of the top oil producers in the world (currently ranked 13). So, stock up while you are there.

Kazakhstan is a good vacation spot for the Jews.

(Sources: Stephen Roth Institute, ADL.org and findlocalweather.com.)

1492

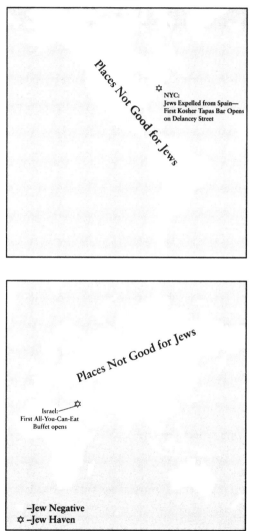

1897

2006

NYC :
"Yes, But Is It Good for the Jews?"
Becomes Rallying Call for
Hillary Clinton's Run for
President

Guess What? Still Not that Good for Jews

Israel:
Sharon Achieves Lifetime Ambition—
Hamas Governs Palestine

– Jew Negative
 – Jew Haven

VIAGRA 'Viagra is a prescription medicine taken by mouth for the treatment of erectile dysfunction (ED) in men. ED is a condition where the penis does not harden and expand when a man is sexually excited, or when he cannot keep an erection. Viagra may help a man with ED get and keep an erection when he is sexually excited.' (Source: US Federal Drug Agency.)

◆ ◆ ◆

The Jewish attitude towards the sexual act has long been the butt of jokes. A religious couple about to marry ask their rabbi if they are allowed to dance together at weddings. 'Categorically, *no*,' says the rabbi. 'What about sex? Are the rules as harsh once we are married?' 'You must have sex! It's a mitzvah,' the rabbi replies. 'Different positions?' they timidly ask. 'Absolutely, in fact the Torah commands the Jewish man to pleasure the Jewish woman at all times.' 'Even doggie position?' 'Whatever you want.' 'Woman on top?' 'Why not?' the rabbi responds without flinching. 'Standing up?' the couple ask. 'Absolutely not!' the rabbi shouts. 'Why ever not?' the young man asks. 'It might lead to dancing,' the rabbi replies.

Now that Jewish couples have had the good news that Viagra is kosher for Passover (a ruling in 1998 allowed its use after some discussion over whether the coating of the pills was non-kosher), in Israel a prescription for Viagra, according to BBC News, is issued once every minute. That rabbis encourage congregants to use the wonder drug is because procreation is good for the Jews. No surprise, then, to discover that one of the key scientists behind its invention at Pfizer was a Jew called Robert Furchgott.

As we've said, Jews and sex are strange bedfellows. There are many jokes about how rare the act is in Jewish homes, and yet the evidence is otherwise. Jews have always played a large part in the adult film industry in America. Reuben Sturman, the 'Disney of double penetration', was a notorious purveyor of filth, controlling a large part of the industry in the seventies; Steven Hirsch runs Vivid Entertainment Group, the Paramount of porn; and Seymore Butts (Adam Glasser) owns and operates the top indie brand, the Miramax of masturbation. These are just three Jewish pioneers in this much-maligned business. Without Viagra to encourage performers, where would this vital Jewish business be?

Before you rush out to order a dozen more packets of Viagra, please remember there are side effects. Priapism, or constant erection, is not so funny. Nor is diarrhoea. Do not take on Kol Nidre.

---

backlash + impact x j-factor = tzurus ÷ kabbalah = good/not good
3.2   + 6.9   x 6   = 60.6 ÷ 7   = 8.7

 VIAGRA IS GOOD FOR THE JEWS.

WIMBLEDON TENNIS CHAMPIONSHIPS

An annual event that lasts for two weeks every June in the borough of Merton in south-west London (population 38,192). The tournament went from a small 'garden party' gathering in 1877 with a few hundred onlookers to the most important lawn tennis competition in the world with over 500,000 international visitors plus millions of television viewers.

✦   ✦   ✦

The All England Lawn Tennis Club, the organization that runs the tournament, has not always been as inclusive an institution as its title proclaims.

When Brit Angela Buxton won the Wimbledon Doubles Championship of 1956 with American Althea Gibson, their victory did not result in the traditional invitation to join the exclusive All England Lawn Tennis Club. Perhaps their forehand lobs were not developed enough for inclusion on the prestigious membership list. Or could it be because they were Jewish and black? Fifty years on, the invitation has not arrived on Ms Buxton's doormat.

Tennis and the Jews have an uneasy relationship. In

May 2005, during the Qatar Total German Open Tennis Tournament (yes, it had to be in Germany), an article in the annual programme featured nostalgic photos of Hermann Goering at Berlin's Rot-Weiss Club. It went on to describe the war years as the club's 'golden age'. Ah, those happy, *Judenfrei* years . . .

On a brighter note, there have been some Jewish success stories at Wimbledon. Dick Savitt was the first Jewish champion, winning the men's singles title in 1951 (although he did beat fellow Jew Herb Flam in the semis, which is a bit of a shame).

Several other Jewish tennis players have competed at Wimbledon (Jonathan Erlich, Brian Gottfried, Pierre Darmon, Anna Smashnova, et al.) but Richard Raskin (aka Renee Richards) must win the prize for being the most versatile, having played in both the men's and women's pro tour. Yes, Renee 'swings both ways'. Raskin underwent a sex-change operation, and the New York Supreme Court granted her the right to play in the women's tour in 1977. Richards returned to opthalmology after her tennis career ended. Much more sensible job for a nice Jewish boy, I mean girl.

---

backlash + impact x j-factor = tzurus ÷ kabbalah = good/not good

2.2   + 4.5   x 2.1   = 14.07 ÷ 7   = 2.01

✳ WIMBLEDON IS NOT GOOD FOR THE JEWS.

WINDSOR, HENRY (PRINCE HARRY) Prince Henry – always known as Prince Harry – is third in line of succession to the throne, behind his father, the Prince of Wales, and his elder brother, Prince William. In September 1998 Harry started at Eton College, Windsor, and ended up with two A-levels: Art (B) and Geography (D). Prince Harry then left England to spend the first part of his gap year in Australia and then went to Africa, where he worked in an orphanage in Lesotho. In May 2005 Prince Harry entered the Royal Military Academy Sandhurst to begin his training as an officer in the army. On 5 July 2005, Prince Harry was cleared of cheating on his Art A-level.

✦   ✦   ✦

On 8 January 2005, Harry attended a fancy-dress party on the theme of 'Colonials and Natives' at a country estate in Wiltshire. Mmm . . . what could the third in line to the throne of England wear? Ceremonial robes from an old family wardrobe? Something from the Tudors, perhaps? Oh, I know, a MILITARY TUNIC with a GERMAN FLAG on the arm and a SWASTIKA armband.

Now, fancy-dress parties can be clear indicators of subconscious activity, and it must be a matter of the utmost gravity when a member of the Royal Family enjoys his Saturday night kitted out as a member of the Wehrmacht.

However, the timing of this outrageous act of poor taste was perfect for the Jewish community. For, two weeks later, the British commemoration of the sixtieth anniversary of the liberation of Auschwitz was due to take place and otherwise might have gone unnoticed, were it not for the furore created by Prince Harry's whimsical choice of outfits. This must surely be seen as a good act for the Jews? However, his choice to take his gap year in Australia and Lesotho and not on a kibbutz in northern Israel must be viewed dimly. Rumours abound on the internet about a possible pending paternity suit, and for this reason alone Judologists should note an unusually high J-factor for a member of the Royal Family.

---

backlash + impact x j-factor = tzurus ÷ kabbalah = good/not good
6.8   + 5.22   x 1.79   = 21.52 ÷ 7   = 3.07

✳ PRINCE HARRY IS NOT GOOD FOR THE JEWS.

XMAS Christmas is a Christian festival which falls on 25 December and celebrates the birth of Jesus. It is generally accepted that Jesus was not actually born on this day, and some theologians believe the festival was established at this time of year to coincide with the pagan winter solstice, thereby encouraging pagans to accept Christ as the Lord.

*   *   *

A happy time for most people, Christmas is also hugely important to the health of a nation's economy. Most retailers develop their whole marketing strategy around the run-up period to Christmas, and profits are dictated by customer spend in the gift-purchasing period from Halloween to Christmas. Hollywood is also geared up to this festive season. Interestingly, as Tom Teicholz pointed out in the *Jewish Journal of Los Angeles*, many seasonal blockbusters have been conceived and produced by Jews. *Elf* (2004), directed and written by and starring Jews (Jon Favreau, David Berenbaum, James Caan, Edward Asner), grossed over $150 million. Perhaps the most famous Jewish Christmas movie is *White Christmas* (1954, dir. Michael Curtiz, written Norm Krasna and starring

Danny Kaye). Only fitting, really, considering it is a celebration of the World's Most Famous Jew.

Christmas is also a good time for Jewish identity. To be able to say boldly to work colleagues, 'Oh, I'm not doing anything for Christmas. I'm Jewish,' often wins gasps of admiration, loathing and slight envy. A re-action most Jews are used to by now.

The commercialization of Christmas has led to the commercialization of Hanukkah – not a good thing for Jews. Don't forget, Jews have to buy eight presents for the eight days of the festival. No longer can a parent get away with a doughnut and a pound coin, but there are only so many PlayStation III games a Jew can afford. Mind you, we should spare a thought for those poor followers of Jews for Jesus who get hit for both holi-days. Ouch.

This commercialization of religion does come at a price.

A Jewish turkey farmer goes to the Vatican and promises a donation of £50 million if the pope will change the Lord's prayer to 'Give us this day our daily turkey'. The pope refuses. He raises the offer to £75 million. Still no. Finally, he leaves an offer of £100 mil-lion on the table. The next day, the pope announces to the Vatican Assembly some good news and some bad news. 'Good news: we have received £100 million from an anonymous donor. Bad news: we have lost the Hovis account.'

Perhaps the best description of Jews' experience at Christmas is movingly portrayed in the classic song

'The Lonely Jew on Christmas' (*South Park*). In the *Judology Quarterly Review*, Solomon Pinkas wrote of the lyrics: 'an excoriating critique of Christmas as seen by a young Jewish infant. Each year, while his chimney goes ignored, the boy is stuck lighting candles, night after night, and forced to suffer the indignities of eating kosher latkes instead of traditional hams. A devastating exploration of the true Hebrew condition at Christmas – the Jew is reduced to loneliness and self-absorption' (*JQ*, Paranoid Publications).

---

backlash + impact x j-factor = tzurus ÷ kabbalah = good/not good
5.2   + 6.8   x 6.1   = 73.2 ÷ 7   = 10.4

 XMAS IS GOOD FOR THE JEWS.

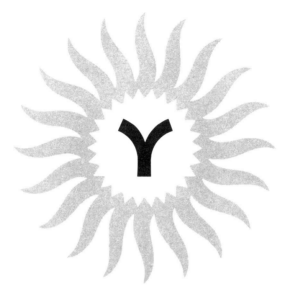

YES, BUT IS IT GOOD FOR THE JEWS? First published by Bloomsbury in America and by Penguin in the UK in 2006, this 'beginner's guide' revealed the secrets of Judology to the unsuspecting public. The determination of whether something or somebody is good for the Jews caused some controversy and the book was publicly burned in parts of Brooklyn and Golders Green. It was not stocked in several bookshops for fear of reprisals. This was later to be revealed as a publicity stunt.

❖   ❖   ❖

Bloomsbury US and Penguin UK, the publishing companies behind this book, do, remarkably, employ non-Jews, which proves that there is diversity in publishing as opposed to Hollywood. The acquiring editors involved with this edition are not Jews (they're Roman Catholic and Church of England) and therefore cannot be blamed for publishing this book, which some have already described as 'cynical religious pornography' (*Der Yidisher Tam Tam*, Paris, 2006).

'*Is it good for the Jews?*' is a common phrase used even among non-Jews. Corporate executives, for example, have been heard to ponder the wisdom of certain strategic decisions with the question, 'Yes, but is it good for the Jews?' In other words, is it going to suit our narrow, focused goals and will it do us harm? For semioticians among you, the phrase is code for 'Let's face it, everyone is out to get us, so before proceeding, let's check if this is going to play badly for us.'

Judology is a pseudo-science with no explanation of how the scoring is determined, which renders the entire exercise highly dubious. Rumours have floated on the internet that the author is a member of the extreme right JANGFY movement (Jews Are Not Good For You), which went underground after the first edition outsold *The Da Vinci Code* by two to one in its first week on the shelves. The publishers simply refer to the author, whom they've never met, as 'Deep Jew'.

Is this concept a narrow-minded and parochial view from a paranoid people which typifies all that is wrong with modern-day Jews? Or is it a necessary reminder that Jews must be on guard at all times to detect danger in everyday life? Either way, do you have to shout about it so?

You decide:

---

backlash + impact x j-factor = tzurus ÷ kabbalah = good/not good

? + ? x ? = ? ÷ 7 = ?

ZOOLATRY Put simply, the worship of one's pet animal(s).

❖ ❖ ❖

Jews are prohibited from walking their dogs on the Sabbath or pulling them on leashes on the Day of Rest, so it is not surprising that, traditionally, Jews have not been huge dog owners. Who needs the mishegoss of jerking little Rover to shul? Also, there is a law that does not allow adults to eat before their dog has. Enough said? (Forget Shabbos, what about Yom Kippur? Rover hasn't had to stay in shul all day breathing in everyone else's halitosis).

Under Jewish law dogs have the same rights as humans and therefore are commanded to rest on Sabbath and holy days. No switching channels as Shabbos Goy (or dog).

Jews might not have pets (frumer Jews have lots of children, which amounts to the same thing), but Jewish law and tradition look very kindly on animals. In fact, unlike Christianity and most civilizations until 1800, Judaism has always outlawed cruelty to animals. Remember, Jacob, Moses and David were all shepherds; in fact, Moses got his job as leader of the

Jews because of his skill in caring for animals: 'Since you are merciful to the flock of a human being, you shall be the shepherd of My flock, Israel' (The Talmud).

Jews and dogs go back a long way. There is a midrash (Tanchumah), according to pupsforpeace.org, that tells the rather gruesome story of what happened after the Red Sea drowned the duped Egyptians: 'Each Jew took his dog, and went to the body of an Egyptian, putting his foot on the Egyptian's throat. He then said to his dog, "Eat the hand that enslaved me!"' Thus, the Jews had dogs, and they left in the Exodus along with the Jews.'

This blind love of the pet can go too far. For example, the recent phenomenon of the 'bark mitzvah'. A rabbi starts with the blessing said when seeing beautiful animals and ends the ceremony by awarding a bark mitzvah certificate to the dog's owner. I suppose an arts scroll series is a step too far.

Kindness to animals has extended to the Middle Eastern conflict. In 2005, after the withdrawal from Gaza, many pets were left in the ruined former settlers' residencies. Tali Lavie, a spokesperson for Hakol Chai (an animal-related legislation lobby group), says Israelis believe the pets are 'brave disengagement dogs'. A similar sentiment has often been expressed by the Palestinian leadership, except perhaps omitting the word 'brave' and referring to their owners.

backlash + impact x j-factor = tzurus ÷ kabbalah = good/not good
4.4   + 3.5   x 6.8   = 53.72 ÷ 7   = 7.67

☀ ZOOLATRY IS BORDERLINE AND THEREFORE NOT GOOD FOR THE JEWS.

ACKNOWLEDGEMENTS

Firstly I would like to thank my wife Karen for her love, support and unstinting belief in this project, but I can't – she was dead against it.

On a lighter note. I am indebted to the Great Karen Rinaldi and all at Bloomsbury for taking the risk on this book and especially the brilliant Yelena 'kosher tattoo' Gitlin and Colin 'three out of four' Dickerman for their advice, belief and expertise. Many thanks to Helen Conford and all the team at Penguin Press too. Special thanks to Claire 'research is my middle name' Berliner for her brilliance and cheers to all my colleagues at Curtis Brown (Doug Kean, Alice Lutyens and Viv Schuster especially), who tolerated the repeated printing of this manuscript on company time. Thank you Anna Davis, who took the poisoned chalice of representing me and taught an old dog some new tricks.

A special thanks to all the authors I represent, for politely turning a blind eye to this strange project of mine.

As with all Jews, I owe most of the material in this book to my family. They may not have known it, but I learnt to view everything from the fall of Margaret Thatcher to the price of apples in terms of whether or not it was good for the Jews. Their humour, love and support have allowed me to bring their name into such disrepute with this book, and for that I thank the Gellers – Mum, Dad, Phil and Rich. Special thanks must go to Andrew Mattison, the source of some fantastic jokes (and dreadful ones too) and to Charlotte Mendelson and Claire Tisne, Geoff Kloske, Bruce Tracy, Greg Williams, David Hirshey, Richard Charkin and Toby Mundy for their early enthusiasm.

My family of friends that began with Habonim all those years ago must be thanked, as those late-night debates about whether gefilte fish did in fact improve sperm counts proved invaluable: so a big thank you to Marshall Yarm, Adam Goldwater, Jonny Mendelson, Jonny Gould, Manuel Harlan and all who contributed in some way to this book. Jonny Marks and Jonny Freedland are more Jonnys who deserve my gratitude. Marks is a number one mensch/friend and Freedland is a great mentor and fantastic friend, and I hope he enjoyed seeing his consigliere turning to him for advice for once.

Oh, all right, Karen, thank you, doll.

PERMISSIONS

Lyrics from *Joseph and the Amazing Technicolor Dreamcoat* reprinted by kind permission of Tim Rice. Copyright © Tim Rice, 1968.

Illustration of the Jewish Nose reprinted by kind permission of Ross Woodrow of the University of Newcastle, taken from George Jabet's *Notes on Noses* (London, 1852).

Every effort has been made to trace copyright holders. The publishers are happy to correct any omissions in future editions.